A GOD DREAM

RECOGNIZING HOW TO MAXIMIZE GOD'S WILL AND MINIMIZE YOUR WISH

E. DEWEY SMITH

To Vivian May God Bless & Keep You!

E Dewey

"Coleman Love"

ISBN: 978-0-9857849-5-9

Printed in the United States of America.

Library of Congress Cataloging-in-Publication Data

A God Dream-Recognizing How to Maximize God's Will And Minimize Your Wish

E. Dewey Smith, Jr. (1970)

Unless otherwise indicated, Scripture quotations are taken from The King James Version of the Bible, public domain.
Scripture quotations marked MSG are taken from THE MESSAGE. Copyright © by Eugene H. Peterson 1993, 1994, 1995, 1996, 2000, 2001, 2002. Used by permission of NavPress Publishing Group.

Cover, book, and interior design by KDR Consulting, LLC ®

Published By MarkOne Publishing
3645 Marketplace Blvd, Suite 130-370
Atlanta, Georgia 30344
A subsidiary of KDR Consulting, LLC

Dedications

*This book is dedicated to my late grandfathers,
Pastor Jack Smith, Jr. and Deacon Elijah Fields, Sr.,
whose example, humility, and spirituality are
foundational to my very being.
It is also dedicated to the late Dr. Willie L. Reid, Sr.,
a man who befriended me when I was eighteen years old.
Dr. Reid ably served as my consistent mentor,
counselor, confidante and example until trading
in the mortal for the immortal.*

To God be the glory for these great human beings.

CONTENTS

PREFACE

S ometimes the plans you have for your life do not reflect God's will or purpose for you.

Life-altering visions come to those who can discern His voice and who are conscious of His presence. They are smeared with the proverbial oil of blessings and are hand-picked to further the Kingdom of God. Dreams are designed by God to come *to* you and be manifested *through* you.

Don't misunderstand. I'm not talking about those weird scenarios that show up in the middle of the night after you've feasted close to bedtime on Thai, Indian, or soul food. That's indigestion, not inspiration. (Though it is not unlike God to wake you up at 3:00 A.M. with an amazing, impactful business idea that will benefit others and prosper you at the same time.) Likewise, the dreams discussed in this book are not what appear in your subconscious after you have watched a nightmare-inducing movie filled with vampires and meat cleavers. (We may need to discuss disciplining yourself in terms of what you eat and what you allow to enter into your spirit, but I digress.)

In particular, I want to bring your thoughts to the kind of dreams that, when manifested, will bring blessings to all who are touched by them and reveal the glory of God's touch.

This is the Genesis story of Joseph. God planted, watered, and caused Joseph's life's dream to blossom in the midst of trouble and chaos, and… in spite of the fact that this man of the Bible was a tad sloppy in his personal dealings, God's permissive will allowed it temporarily before his dreams manifested. Joseph was, for a time, the opposite of decent and orderly. You may be in that space right now as well, but hold on — God is not finished with you (or the dreams He has planted within you).

Joseph, son of Jacob, grandson of Isaac, great-grandson of Abraham, was the reflection of God's promises, which we can view through the mirror of Scripture. God imbued Joseph with a dream that appeared to others to be lofty and unreachable, but turned out to be the saving grace of him and everyone connected with him. And since God is no respecter of persons, you already know that if He did it for Joseph, He can and will do it for you! God's perfect will is for you to follow His divine plan for your life. He has given His word as an instructional manual on how to live the best life possible.

Remember, if it's in the Word, it can materialize in your world! But like anything worth doing, there is an order — steps, if you will — to getting to where God would have you be.

ABRAHAM, ISAAC, AND JACOB

Let's journey through biblical background in Genesis so that we may focus on what God has in store in this present day. Why? Because we can only get where we're going if we know where we, as Christians, have been, and what the Lord has brought us through. The final destination, and the goal of this book, is to bring you to a place where you can discern whether the lifelong dreams you've been nursing and rehearsing truly line up with the plan God has for your life.

Joseph's lineage begins with Abraham and can be traced down to Jesus. While Abraham (Abram, before God anointed him) was in Ur, the land of the Chaldees, God told him that if he followed directions and ventured where the Lord was leading him, his offspring would be *"like the stars of heaven in number,"* (Deuteronomy 1:10). He promised that in Abraham's seed all the earth would be blessed, and, as you know, Abraham ultimately became known as 'the father of many nations'. This Bible great is a perfect example of how when you have faith in what God tells you it will indeed come to pass.

So, of all the characters found and stories told in the Bible, why Joseph? Well, first of all, Abraham's lineage is rife with those whose belief system and trust in God can successfully be applied to our own lives. Joseph is the personification of God-given dreams that come to fruition to the joy and happiness of all involved. Joseph's dream propelled him to great heights and brought him to the place God had intended him to reach all along. It was a gift from God, and it ultimately brought him before great men. Your dreams, when manifested, will do the same.

Now, the dream Joseph had was in no way attached to some fantasy world but was aligned with God's purpose and plan for his life. He was 17 years old when his dream initially came up in his spirit, which is significant because this means Joseph's destiny was pre-ordained. It confirmed that his place in the world (as well as yours) was established by God early on. It's your job to find out what He would have you do, and take the proper steps to reach that divine place.

Maybe you're asking yourself, "What if I'm well past my teenage years and still don't know exactly what the Lord would have me do?" The simple answer is: All you need to do is ask God in prayer what marvelous way He created you to be a blessing. Each of us was born for a special, divine purpose.

Each of us has been given the spiritual and intellectual tools to carry out whatever God has called us to do. If you haven't figured out your divine purpose, or if you've already asked and still haven't gotten an answer, remember this: *"If any of you lacks wisdom, you should ask God, who gives generously to all without finding fault, and it will be given to you, "* (James 1:5). You may need to candidly ask yourself what you're doing that is hindering your ability to hear from the Lord.

What about your dreams? Do you daydream while you're waiting in traffic or sitting for hours on end waiting to see the doctor? Do you ever dream so vividly that you have to scan the room to confirm your whereabouts? Do you know if your dream to be an acclaimed chef, or the world's fastest runner or to own an international chain of childcare centers comes from your desire to be famous or from God with the intention of easing your fellow man's burdens?

I'm sure you remember your grandmother lovingly telling you that when you dream of fish (who does that?) it's because someone close to you is pregnant. If you daydream that your hand itches, God is about to bless you with a wad of cash. Perhaps these really mean you need to turn off the television hours before going to bed or invest in some good lotion. But all joking aside, every dream that comes to you is not necessarily of God.

How do you really know if your dream is attached to God's purpose? What are the criteria to help you determine that your dream is not solely for self-aggrandizement but is meant to bless others? Just because you think or even passionately believe something does not mean it's from Him. The fish dream and the itching hands superstition make for lighthearted stories around the dinner table, but they don't inspire you to change your life and, ultimately, the world. While it's okay to seek out the meaning of that type of thought, your time is better spent searching out God's purpose for your life.

Those lightweight dreams, which contain perhaps a hint of your personal agenda, are not in the same league as the ones Dr. Martin Luther King, Jr. (MLK) spoke about in August of 1963 while sponsoring the famous March on Washington (D.C.) to promote civil rights. At that time, he gave what many consider to be one of the most important speeches of the twentieth century. He envisioned living in a nation where his children would be judged not by the color of their skin, but by the content of their character. Indeed, this dream exemplified MLK's lifetime pursuits, and as an added benefit, planted the seeds of social justice, racial equality, and freedom for all in this country. It's important that you are able to distinguish between personal ambition, untamed thoughts, and what is truly the call of God on your life.

The Difference Between Ambition and Anointing

There is a difference between a dream that comes out of your ambition and one that comes from the anointing. Many of us have dreams and ambitions, but they do not necessarily come from God. When you have an intimate relationship with God, it is your responsibility to discuss His plans for your life during your intimate moments of devotion.

You *have* not because you *ask* not. If you are still unsure of what God wants you to do, where He wants you to be, and, in fact, who He wants you to be with, all you have to do is ask. He does not want you to be ignorant of your place in the world, so your discernment between your ambition and His anointing is vital. Why? Because even Christians can mistake personal ambition for the will of the Father.

The following is a case in point and is clearly exaggerated for illustrative purposes, but you'll know exactly where I'm going with this. You may dream of being the next pop icon. But you and everyone within earshot knows that you can't carry a tune in a bucket. You have no flair for the dramatic or sense of what's entertaining. Besides all of that, you don't take rejection well. That's vital, since your pipe dream song won't always be at the top of the charts. In this instance, you may be confusing your preference with God's purpose. Remember, just because you have those ambitions does not mean that is the lot God has assigned to you.

The Bible tells us that if we delight ourselves in the Lord, He will give us the desires of our hearts. Some hear 'He will give us the *desires* of our hearts,' while others hear 'He will *give* us the desires of our hearts.' It's a matter of emphasis. Clearly, it's a matter of translation and, possibly, semantics.

And while that concept is taken directly from Scripture, your interpretation will dictate whether or not you align your dreams with a personal desire or trust it to be something given to you from the Lord.

Reality has to do with the difference between the selfish desires of your heart and what He has predestined. As a Christian who trusts God, your heart's desires should always be secondary to the revelation of God's purpose in your life. If the desires of your heart don't line up with His Word (which is the foundation for what He has ordained), your prayer, in the name of Jesus, should be:

> "God, don't just give me the desires of my heart, but also give me the revelation of Your will and assignment for me. And then, once You reveal my assignment, allow my ambitions to line up with what You've assigned for my life. This I pray in Jesus' name."

Are you where you feel you should be? Are you content with the choices you have made? One reason you may not be making the progress you feel you should have made at this stage of your life is that your personal ambition and divine assignment do not match. It may well be that your ambitions are diametrically opposed to your divine assignment. God may be pulling your heart in one direction, while you're running, kicking and screaming, the opposite way.

The Bible tells us that hope deferred makes the heart sick. That said, you will become frustrated when you feel as if your ambitions are not being realized. What may actually be occurring is that your frustration is directly related to the fact that God's assignment for you is not presently being realized.

Ask yourself, "Am I living based on what I want to do or on what God wants me to do?" If you're not living according to God's plans, you will be perpetually battling within your spirit, and you will not have the peace that the Bible tells you surpasses all understanding.

God knows from the beginning, before we're born, what His plan is for us. We just have to line our spirit up with His so that we can know, too. At the church where I am senior pastor, The Greater Travelers Rest Baptist Church in Decatur, Georgia, we perform baby dedications for infants and toddlers. We present our children to God the way the Bible's Hannah did with her son, Samuel. We believe that children aren't mature enough to make the quality decision to be baptized or to know what 'sayeth the Lord God of Hosts' where their young lives are concerned. Since we are well aware of a child's decision-making limitations and an inability to know what God wants them to do, we stand in the gap with this prayer:

"God, early on in the lives of these children, please reveal their purpose to their parents so that they, along with grandparents, aunts, and uncles, can help push them in the direction they should go, so when they get older, they will not depart from it. This we ask in Jesus' name. Amen."

Once you know what God has ordained for your life, you can take proper steps toward getting there and getting on with it. Joseph was anointed and appointed, but early on in his life he was definitely not aware. But, child of God, don't you know that when God gives vision, He makes provision?

Genesis 37 begins with God *giving* Joseph a dream. God anointed him with a specific task that, upon further reading, you will see lay somewhat dormant until the set time when Joseph was positioned to realize what God had implanted in his heart. This is a dream that our study shows he never asked for or thought about previously. He was clearly appointed. Nowhere in Scripture do we see that anyone else had the same dream.

Ironically, Joseph didn't even understand it at the time. However, God used this dream to plant the seeds in Joseph, designating what he would eventually become and who he would eventually be. God handed Joseph a glimpse of his destiny and Egypt's future.

Is your dream spirit-borne or self-centered? Did you come to it on your own, or was it planted by God in your spirit? Has God shown you your future? Are you operating presently in what you heard from God in the past?

You will have a problem discerning the source of your desires as long as you are out of order with the things of God. If you're going to receive and ultimately accept the dream, you must get your spiritual house in order. This will ensure that when God anoints you with a plan for your life that will bless others, you will be 'meet' (suitable) for the Master's use. What God has for you *is* for you, and once you acknowledge His plan, no one can stop it from coming to pass. Even though Joseph's life before the manifestation was untidy, God blessed him anyway.

When you read the account of Joseph and his brothers, you may be inclined to think they mistreated him. He told them about his dream, and out of jealousy, or frustration, or both, they began to plan all kinds of mischief where he was concerned. Yet Joseph got into tacky situations not just because of his brothers' reaction to him, but also because of his reaction to the world around him. As the old folks are known to say, he helped make his bed hard and then had to lie in it. Joseph himself delayed the materialization of his dream. In effect, he got in his own way. If you take heed to the ways in which Joseph was his own worst enemy, you can judge your life accordingly. Learn what Joseph did wrong so that you can allow God to order your steps toward where He ultimately wants you to be.

You dream. I dream. We all dream. But if you know God's Word, you won't be responsible for delaying the manifestation of His plan for your life.

Resolve to be Decent and in Order

Joseph led a life of disorder.

Genesis 37:2 (MSG) says, *"This is the story of Jacob. The story continues with Joseph, seventeen years old at the time, helping out his brothers in herding the flocks. These were his half-brothers actually, the sons of his father's wives Bilhah and Zilpah. And Joseph brought his father bad reports on them."*

Jacob fathered a dozen sons, all of whom were responsible for working out in the field and herding and tending their father's flock of sheep. Whenever they came back in from work, Joseph would go into his father's chamber and tattle about his brothers' activities, or lack thereof. He did this daily. Maybe someone should have told him that going about as a talebearer is ungodly and out of order.

When God appoints and anoints you and you allow your spirit to be infused with His plan for your life, you must become aware of your surroundings and awaken to His voice. You have to understand the part you play in the manifestation of your dream. You need to let all things be done decently and in order, and that includes the way you treat others. Often you may fall into the trap of spending time watching what others are doing or trying to figure out who is blessed and who is not. But when you are worrying about what everyone else is doing, you dilute the power of God to use you because you aren't properly concentrating on your particular assignment. You aren't allowing yourself to be consecrated to that which God would have you do.

Have you ever noticed that there are those who think they've been specifically appointed for the sole purpose of throwing others under the bus? They stir up trouble and insinuate themselves into the middle of messy situations. And afterward, these same infantile troublemakers act as if they had nothing to do with the unfolding chaos. Have you been told that everything is peaceful in your workplace when you're not there? Has anyone ever said that whenever you come to work all kinds of craziness breaks out in the office? Am I talking about you? If so, perhaps you're like Joseph who created a hostile environment by snitching on his brothers. Talk about sibling rivalry and dysfunction! If you fancy yourself a dreamer, and more importantly, one whose dreams are blessed by the Creator, then you will have to live a life of forgiveness, compassion, and concern for others. You can't be messy in your personal or professional endeavors.

You Don't Have to Tear Others Down

Joseph was a dreamer, and it was obvious that his father adored him. On the face of things, maybe Jacob doted on this son to the exclusion of the others. In order to gain his father's favor, this dreamer resorted to consistently showing his brothers in the worst light possible. This wasn't good for Joseph and his brothers, and it was certainly a harbinger of problems to come in their relationship. Joseph appeared to be alienating himself from his brothers, 'cruising for a bruising' from eleven healthy, strong young men. If, by constant snitching, Joseph's plan was to curry his dad's favor, well, things worked out just fine for him, at least at the time.

"So let's agree to use all our energy in getting along with each other. Help others with encouraging words; don't drag them down by finding fault." (Romans 14:19 MSG)

Hear me out, child of God. If tearing down others is what you did to attain what you perceive as your lofty place, then tearing down others is what you're going to have to keep doing to stay up on that high horse. On top of that, you may want to prepare yourself for the eventual tumble that will inevitably come. There's always talk about reaping what you sow, but that's not entirely true. You reap *more* than you sow. Payback seems to multiply somehow.

My advice is that you not use unfair means to gain merit on your behalf. If God has a dream for your life, it precludes interfering with others and always trying to figure out what they are doing. God knows who you are, where you are, and how to find you. When God has a divine mandate or assignment for your life, it matters not who may appear to be better qualified, more experienced, or whether they're the boss' golf partner. Nothing can prevent you from getting to the place God has for you, as long as you operate in faithfulness. Of course, you can stop what God has in store if you choose to walk in foolishness.

While I'm on the subject of tearing others down, I understand that the corporate environment can be rather cutthroat. That proverbial dog-eat-dog mentality usually permeates most business offices. However, you can still protect yourself by making sure you have everything in order. Cover your tracks with a paper trail and make sure to dot your i's and cross your t's. When God reveals His purpose and the place where He wants you to be, no one can destroy what He wants to do in your life. You just need to trust God and be faithful to that concept.

It's too bad Joseph didn't know enough to follow that advice. Nowhere does it say in Scripture that his father wanted him to be in charge of telling on his brothers. The relationship Jacob had with Joseph was in part based on the fact that Jacob fathered him late in life.

And then there was that coat. The Bible says it was elaborately embroidered, but are you thinking like I'm thinking… that 'gaudy' may have been a better word to describe it? Not to add a jot or tittle to the Word, but I'm just saying. Because Jacob gave Joseph a coat that stood out, it no doubt reminded the other eleven sons that their father had a habit of showing favoritism toward this particular son, favoritism that wasn't equally dispersed among the other eleven siblings. Maybe, just maybe, Jacob was partly responsible for Joseph's lack of order and the resulting mess he made of his life. That is of course, until the dreamer's dreams were realized. But I'm getting ahead of myself.

If you're a parent, imagine how your children would feel if you blatantly favored one over the other. It's no surprise that siblings turn to rivalry because one feels that he or she is not loved as much as the next one. Parents should be especially careful not to allow the youngest in the family to get away with behavior and privileges that the older children didn't have — staying up late, talking back, or other behaviors that the earlier children were disciplined for.

I know it's not politically correct to say this, but some children these days get away with attitudes and actions that we would have been chastised for. As a parent, you should strive to not show favoritism like Jacob did. You may feel closer to one child and love another child in a different way. In my mind, parents should make a concerted effort to never do more for one child than another. Now, you may want to reward your child based on achievement or merit, but as a basic practice, you should strive to be fair with all of your children.

Reading further, we see Genesis 37:4: *"Now when the brothers saw that their father loved him more than them, they hated him and could not speak peaceably unto him."*

Notice that now Joseph's brothers recognize this obvious partiality, and as a result, they're not even talking to him in a civil manner. Joseph goes about showing off his colorful coat. He is aware that he is the only one of the brothers who received such a gift from Jacob. If this happened today, he'd be the only one with a new bicycle, and he'd be riding around while the others were walking, ringing the bell as he rode past, and gloating. That's probably how his brothers felt. It finally dawned on them that Jacob was not treating them properly.

And Joseph dreamed a dream.

He told the dream to the same brothers he'd been throwing under the bus. They were already angry with him, and now he added insult to injury by not just sharing, but bragging about his vision. His brothers realized during the recounting of this dream that yet again, they were at the bottom of Jacob's totem pole. The Bible says that they hated him — harsh, but totally understood.

Now, let's revisit earlier Scripture. We found out that Joseph was a teenager when the first dream initially came to him, which means he was plenty old enough to know he was causing friction with his brothers. He knew they had a problem with him. In fact, the Bible says they hated him. It's kind of hard for Joseph not to have at least an inkling of their contempt. Do you want your godly dreams to come to fruition? Then ". . . *if it is possible, as far as it depends on you, live at peace with everyone."* (Romans 12:18 NIV)

Through the recounting of his dream, Joseph confirmed what his brothers already knew — he felt superior to them based on the special treatment he was getting from Jacob.

"We were all out in the field one day, gathering bundles of wheat. And all of a sudden my bundle stood straight up in the air. And your bundles circled around mine and bowed down to mine," (Genesis 37:7). In other words, Joseph was telling them that their sheaves were making obeisance to his sheaves. His brothers wanted to know if he was saying that he was going to be the boss of them. *"And they hated him more than ever because of his dreams and the way he talked."* (Genesis 37:8)

Joseph had another dream. In this one, he told them, ". . . *the sun and moon, and eleven stars bowed down to me."* (Genesis 37:9)

He took things a bit further by telling his father the dream, and he got a response from Jacob that surprised him. His father reprimanded him and questioned whether or not

Joseph actually thought his parents would also bow down to their own son.

Remember to Always Include the Master

The issue here was not with the actual content of Joseph's dream. The dream that he had was indeed from God. There was accuracy and purity with this dream. The real problem with Joseph's dream was that at no time does he ever acknowledge God's hand in the matter. Not once does Joseph indicate how God could be glorified by his dreams; he was too busy lording them over his brothers, as if they originated with him. In that state of mind, all of his dreams were about him and had no connection to God at all.

If your dreams are realized, the first thing to come to mind will be what you can do with the increased finances you'll enjoy as a result of the business idea God planted in your spirit. Will you buy an island? Purchase a Bentley? Travel to exotic places? Or, will you acknowledge that the Lord continually leads you in the paths of righteousness for His name's sake? Hopefully you will pray and ask God how He wants you to glorify Him with the idea He so graciously blessed you with.

Or, what if you win the Powerball? Not that I'm condoning or condemning playing the lottery, but if you are so inclined, one of your first thoughts should be what you can do to help your local church. You should immediately ask what you can do to help the pastor and your fellow churchgoers. No matter what you win, it's more than what you had. And I'm certain that any amount you give to the church will be more than appreciated. Putting others first will almost guarantee you will have enough for the new house, souped up car, and fabulous vacation.

If God isn't being glorified in your business or personal endeavors, they are not worthwhile.

And so, as you can see, Joseph was bragging about his dream but obviously wasn't ready to handle the responsibility that comes with God's blessing.

Recognize That You Need Maturity to Handle the Things of God

Joseph told his brothers about his dreams and they hated him. He told his father about his dreams and ended up insulting him. Further down in the chapter, we're told that his brothers were so full of envy that they plotted to kill him.

> "*They spotted him off in the distance. By the time they got to them they had cooked up a plot to kill him. The brothers were saying, 'Here comes the dreamer. Let's kill him and throw him into one of these old cisterns; we can say that a vicious animal ate him up. We'll see what his dreams amount to.'*" (Genesis 37:18-20 MSG)

It's apparent that Joseph was not mature enough to understand, much less handle, the dreams that came to him. He was not yet prepared for what God was going to do in his life. Because he saw something in the future that he wasn't prepared or mature enough for, he almost ended up getting killed — but for the grace of God.

Are you ready for what God is showing you? Have you ever noticed that athletes and entertainers prosper as a result of the dreams that manifest in their lives? More often than not, their character, maturity, and integrity are not on the same level as either their dreams or their talent.

I've found that money is an amplifier. If you have foolishness in you before you prosper and then get more money to operate in that foolishness, you'll end up living a nightmarish existence. If you operate in whatever dreams God place in your spirit before you are mature enough to handle the role and responsibility, you will no doubt end up stunting what God wants to do in your life.

How do you know that you're not ready? Here are a few clues:

- You dream of owning a business, with all the financial responsibility this entails, but you cannot balance your personal checking account.

- You believe God wants you to pastor your own church, but you neither read the Bible, pray regularly, nor assist in teaching Sunday school.

Let me paraphrase signs of maturity that should be present before you can operate in God's purpose for your life, as stated by a renowned Christian author. You may not be able to operate in the station God wants to assign to you because you haven't yet grasped the difference between what you want for your life and what God wants to do in and with you. How will you know when you're ready or mature enough for the dream to come to fruition?

- For one thing, you (unlike Joseph) will realize that whatever you do is more important for someone else's benefit than your own. Men, you say you are ready to handle a dream marriage, but you're not willing to pull your share of the overall responsibilities of marriage and, ultimately, parenthood. In order for you to consider yourself mature enough to marry and start a family, you must be willing to put your future wife's happiness, comfort, and desires above your own.

- People who are mature in the things of God have what I like to call a discerning spirit. In other words, they can smell trouble a mile away and are not likely to be duped by someone with a slick get-rich-quick scheme.

- I tell the women in my church that most of them should be relationship-savvy enough to know when they are being conned. I try to let them know that at some point their godly discernment should overtake their vulnerability and their (often desperate) desire to be in a relationship. There should come a time in the life of a saved, sold-out-for-Christ female when she can detect that a man means her no good, even before he does or says something that makes it blatantly obvious.

- All of us have heard about, read about, or seen too many shady business deals to allow ourselves to be fooled by crooks. "A fool and his or her money are soon parted," but with the mind of Christ, you should be able to discern whether someone is worthy of a business partnership. If the person trying to corral you into a business venture doesn't have his own place, a checking account, or a car, well . . . those should be ample clues.

- Knowledge is education, street smarts, or a wealth of information. Understanding is the ability to reason. Wisdom is common sense, or the way in which you appropriate the knowledge you've acquired. You need knowledge, discernment, and wisdom before you are ready to fulfill dreams that, up until now, have just been constant thoughts in your mind.

- Many Christians have creative thoughts and ideas, but can they carry through with what they've seen in their minds? Rather than be like some whom I have counseled, who start and stop business ventures at the drop of a hat, I urge those who come to me for advice to devise concrete ideas and stick with them. Get it done.

- Carry your plan to completion. Doing otherwise is an obvious sign of a lack of maturity.

- Temper your emotions with a thorough investment in personal and professional responsibility. In other words, rather than take knee-jerk actions and reactions, take time to think things through.

- Solicit advice and assistance from qualified people.

In January of 2007, my younger brother passed away from Crohn's disease at the age of twenty-eight. Technically, this is a disease that can be managed and is not generally life-threatening, but he did not take good care of himself. He surrounded himself with people whose compassion for him and involvement with what he was going through was apparently not their priority. He didn't have associates who would challenge him to take ownership and care for himself.

Men, don't marry someone who will do anything you say. If you're sick and have high blood pressure, don't marry someone who will bring you fried food every time you ask for it because you're 'the man of the house'. You need a woman who will say, "I'm going to broil this fish for you." You need someone who will love you enough to respectfully disagree with you in order to help you help yourself.

If you already have heart disease and the doctor told you that smoking cigarettes will kill you, you don't want your fiancé buying cigarettes and smoking them with you just because what you say in the home carries a lot of weight. If that's the woman you want, go ahead and marry her. But I promise you this, she will no doubt be very happy when you've passed away and the insurance check comes. I imagine her next husband won't be smoking while he's sleeping in your bed and driving the car that you're not around to drive. You can avoid this situation by helping yourself and by marrying a woman who cares enough to involve herself in what involves you.

A help 'meet and suitable' is a wife who loves you enough to make a doctor's appointment for you and accompany you there for support. Men need someone who will encourage, lift them up, and be there in good times and bad. A woman who watches you live haphazardly while making sure the life insurance policy is paid up is not what you need.

On the other hand, you must take responsibility and get involved to take care of your own needs. You can't smoke three packs of cigarettes a day and then expect folks to pray and care for you. Stop treating loved ones like that. Make yourself and your health a priority, and stop expecting others to care more about your needs than you do. Stop asking God to heal you if you're not willing to be part of the solution. Your needs must be matched by your own self-compassion and self-involvement.

- Practice 'stick-to-it-tiveness'. Sometimes God gives you a dream, but because it hasn't materialized yet, you run away from it. That is not the mature way to handle the situation. Maturity is sticking with what God has shown you until your dream is fulfilled.

- Let change happen. Admit when you've missed the mark, and be ready, willing, and able to make a change. If God has to step in and provide correction to you again and again for the same mistake that means you have some spiritual growing to do.

- When you have the ability to grow spiritually by an independent intake of God's Word, that's a sure sign that you're ready to move forward with what God would have you do.

I can't say this enough. You must understand the difference between human ambition and divine assignment. You have to be willing to put your ambition secondary to what He's assigned you to do. Once God has given you the dream, don't give up on what He's given you to do. He wants to raise your level of maturity to be on the same level as the dream, so that once it materializes you won't mess things up. He doesn't want you to squander the glorious opportunities that your dream holds for you and others.

Child of God, you'll have some hurts in the maturing process. Some of your business partners are going to shank you. It will be painful but necessary. Some people will borrow money and not give it back. All of these disappointments are part and parcel of the process necessary to mature you. Once God's intervention lines up your maturity with the dream, awesome things are in store for you. Believe it, receive it, walk in it, and expect great things in every area of your life.

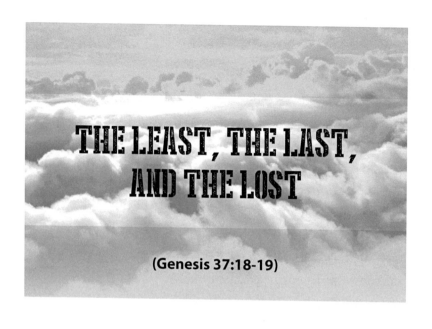

THE LEAST, THE LAST, AND THE LOST

(Genesis 37:18-19)

On January 15, 1929, while his father was pastoring The Greater Travelers Rest Baptist Church on Mayson Avenue in Atlanta, Georgia, Martin Luther King, Jr. was born. He turned out to be such a bright young man that when he was only fifteen he was admitted to Morehouse College in Atlanta, a historically Black university. He distinguished himself as an undergrad by getting involved in several community and extracurricular activities. After his graduation from Morehouse in 1948, he went on to Crozer Theological Seminary, and ultimately to the School of Theology at Boston University.

As a young boy, he was able to view racism firsthand. His father was greatly influenced by the Civil Rights Movement, as well as by Dr. William Holmes Borders, then-pastor of the historic Wheat Street Baptist Church in Atlanta. Martin Luther King, Jr. was influenced by his own father, and also by Dr. Borders, Howard Thurman, Henry David Thoreau, Ghandi, and ultimately Dr. Benjamin Elijah Mays, the President of Morehouse College and his trusted mentor. All of these different perspectives helped develop within him a yearning to play a role in a radically changing American society and, ultimately, the world.

By the time he was twenty-six, Dr. Martin Luther King, Jr. was invited to Montgomery, Alabama to take the helm of pastoral leadership at Dexter Avenue Baptist Church. And as you know, his life came to an untimely end when, at the age of thirty-nine, he was shot and killed while standing on a motel balcony. Dr. King is known for his dream of societal change; it gave him purpose and a reason for being.

You know about Dr. King's life and death, speeches and dreams, struggles and accomplishments. But do you know what *your* dream is? Do you know for what God has fearfully and wonderfully made you to do in this earthly realm? What legacy has He called *you* to leave? What are the priorities that fuel your perspective? What causes you to get up every morning when you don't feel like getting up? What keeps you moving when you feel exhausted?

Have you rightly divined your assignment versus your ambition? Often there is not a clear line of demarcation between what you're ambitious about from a human perspective and what you've been divinely assigned to do.

I bring up Martin Luther King, Jr. and Joseph of the Old Testament because they both possessed life-changing thoughts that had the potential to change the world in which they lived. If we try hard enough, major principles can be gleaned from their lives to help you carry out God's plan for your existence. What assignment has God given you? What happens when you, a dreamer like Joseph and MLK, are ready to come forth? What will transpire when you are ready to actualize your specific dream?

The Dreamer Should Always Receive Priority from the Father

After Joseph dreamed his dream, Genesis 37:12-14 says: *"His brethren went to feed their flocks in Shechem. And Israel [who also was called Jacob] said unto Joseph, 'Do not thy brethren feed the flock in Shechem? Come, and I will send thee unto them.' And he said, 'Here am I.' And he said to him, 'Go, I pray thee, see whether it be well with thy brethren, and well with the flocks; and bring me word again.' So he sent him out of the vale of Hebron, and he came to Shechem."*

In other words, Joseph's father wanted him to bring back a report on his brothers. Look at how clearly the Message Bible renders verse 14: *"Go and see how your flocks and brothers are doing and bring me a report."*

Jacob sent him to the valley of Hebron, in which we find Shechem. Joseph has been instructed by his father to go into the valley and see how his brothers are doing, essentially assigning him as his brothers' keeper. And this priority to oversee, or spy, or check on the state of his brothers' affairs is not coming from Joseph's immaturity or heightened sense of self but is given to him by Jacob as a priority to be taken care of, posthaste.

That, to me, is what the ministry of Dr. Martin Luther King, Jr. was all about. Just as Joseph received instructions and priority from his father, so also did Dr. King receive priority from his heavenly Father, such as:

- "Martin, go and check and see how your brothers (Black) are doing in Montgomery, Alabama, where they are paying the same for goods, services, housing, and transportation as are others (Whites), yet they're not afforded the same rights."

- "Martin, go and check on your sisters. I'm told that a seamstress, Rosa Parks, got on a bus, completely exhausted and her feet hurting, and was told to sit in the back of the bus to give someone else the seat that she paid the same fare for. She was incarcerated due to the laws and ordinances of the city of Montgomery, Alabama. Will you go and see how Rosa Parks is doing?"

- "Martin, will you go to Philadelphia, Mississippi, and check on the civil rights workers who have been killed and buried in a valley, allegedly by law enforcement and members of segregationist hate groups? Martin, will you go and check on your brothers to see how they are doing?"

- "Martin, go and check on Medgar Evers' wife. He was killed in his own front yard for doing that which was pleasing in the sight of the Lord. Martin, go and check on your sister."

- "Martin, go to Montgomery, Alabama. I understand that a local church deacon, who is also employed by the county, may be guilty of turning dogs and fire hoses on those engaging in nonviolent civil protests in that city. Martin, go and check on your brothers there."

- "Martin, go and check on the families of those four little girls who were bombed in that church in Birmingham because they were getting ready to participate in something that was godly and had value. Martin, go and check on those families."

- "Martin, go and check on those boys and girls fighting in Vietnam. They were forced to go over there and fight for the rights of those people, yet within the shores of their own country, some of them don't even have the right to vote. Martin, go and check on them."

- "Martin, go and check on a certain prisoner scheduled for execution here in the South, even when eyewitnesses recanted their statements."

The problem, as I see it, with most 21st century theology is that we've forgotten about our responsibility to go and check on our brothers because our faith is now about individuality, egotism, and narcissism. No one any longer has that holy and righteous indignation to go and check on their brothers and sisters.

Today, I believe that God is saying, "Go and check on your brothers. It's good that some of you have gone from riding in the back of the bus to driving your Mercedes Benz. But when you've stopped checking on your brothers, your faith has lost its realness."

I truly believe that He's telling clergy to:

- "Go and check on your sisters who are doing the same work as men but are overworked and underpaid for the same job."

- "Go and check on those occupying Wall Street and not caring about those on their own street."

- "Go and check on the criminal justice system, and the prison-industrial complex that has privatized the penal system, allowing people to prosper to the detriment of those who are supposed to be rehabilitated in prison. Go and check on your brothers."

- "Go and check on your sisters who are being afflicted with HIV/AIDS, a leading cause of death for women between twenty-five and fifty-four."

- "Go to Camden County, Georgia, and check on your young brothers and sisters, who, under the auspices of public education, were humiliated in a math class. They were given word problems such as, "Each tree had 56 oranges. If eight slaves pick them equally, then how much would each slave pick?" In this day and time, when racism and slavery are still being disguised, you need the holy and righteous indignation to check on your brothers."

• "Go and check on the children who have been molested by preachers and coaches. Make sure they're getting a quality education and after-school programs in a safe environment."

We have to leave our Sunday morning ecclesiastical accoutrements of worship and go out and be concerned about the least of these. God has called us to help, care for, and protect the least, the last, and the lost. If your dream is only for you and you haven't received priority from the Father, your dream will become a nightmare. You've got to ask God, "What am I dreaming for? What am I hoping for? How can others be blessed by what I'm dreaming and hoping for?" If the expectation and manifestation of your dream is only for your health and wealth and you're not concerned about the least, the last, and the lost, then your dream is not of God.

Jesus said the day would come when the sheep and the goats would stand forever and receive their inheritance. *"When I was hungry, you fed Me. I was naked and you clothed Me. I was in jail, and you came to visit Me. When I was sick you came to see about Me. Come and receive the blessing of My Father,"* (Matthew 25:35-36, 34). But to the goats: *"Go and depart from Me to the place of everlasting torment, the place reserved for the Devil and all his angels because you didn't care for Me."* (Matthew 25:41)

The righteous asked, *"Jesus, when did we see You hungry? When did we see You naked? When did we see You in prison? When did we see You outdoors?"* Jesus responded, *"That which you have done to the least of these, My brethren, you've also done it to Me."* (Matthew 25:37-40)

Church, don't rest easy in Zion. Thank God we can go to the sanctuary on Sunday, but we really have to go, worship Him, and then leave to check on our brothers and sisters. We have to make sure — regardless of race, color, creed, socioeconomic status, or whether or not we've judged them as worthy — that we do whatever we can to make sure everyone has the same rights and that justice prevails for all.

You've got to receive a priority from your Father. If everything is just for you and your little group, that doesn't sound to me like what Jesus is about. What have you done for someone else? When was the last time you were a blessing to others? Go and check on your brothers and sisters in Christ.

That's why Dr. King went to Memphis in the first place. Although he was exhausted, he went anyway. He had been to Memphis a few months earlier to stage a boycott and bring interest and attention to the problems there, but things went awry. The meeting and subsequent outcome were not fruitful, but on April 3, 1968, he returned. I'm told that when Dr. King got ready to leave home for Memphis, his son, Martin III, hid his briefcase because he didn't want his father to leave. When his personal assistant came by the house to pick him up, two of Dr. King's children blocked the door and protested more urgently than usual. They did not want their father to leave home that morning, and so the children stood in front of the car and begged their father to stay home. The story goes that Martin III even got up on the hood of the car, pleading with his dad not to leave. He was said to have begged his father to stay home with them and not go away.

Whether fact or urban legend, it has been said that although Dr. King had been on many trips in his life, this was the first time his children had ever acted in that manner. In spite of what he felt and the protests from his children, he flew to Memphis. The following day, he gave the last speech of his life. His purpose in that city was to protest on behalf of sanitation workers who had complained about heinous working conditions. In fact, they felt they were being treated as less than human. During their protest march, they even wore signs that read, "I am a man. Treat me like a man."

Dr. Martin Luther King, Jr. lost his life checking on the welfare, safety, and treatment of his 'brothers'. When was the last time you checked on a brother related not by genealogy but by the human condition? Maybe not through a march or nonviolent protest, but by picking up the phone and saying to someone, "I noticed you were depressed today. I'm just calling to check on you." When was the last time you checked on someone who had lost their job or a loved one, or been through a divorce? When was the last time you checked on a child who didn't have any resources, or who had experienced a death in the family? When was the last time you stopped by just to be a blessing to somebody else? If the whole of your existence and your passion is just yourself, you haven't received priority from the Father. You've got to receive priority, just as Dr. Martin Luther King, Jr. and Joseph with the coat of many colors, did.

Realize That People Will be Frustrated

When you get your dream from God and can clearly ascertain your personal ambition versus your divine assignment, you need to also realize that not everyone will accept what you've heard.

"And when his brothers saw him from afar off, before he came near, they conspired against him to slay him and cast him into a pit." (Genesis 37:18)

It wasn't the Chaldeans or Egyptians or Babylonians who conspired to kill Joseph, but those who grew up in the same home he did. Don't be surprised when people who are close to you hate on you because God has given you revelation for your life. The problem with many of us is that we try to 'dumb down' our dream and assignment so that other people will like and accept us. Don't lose your common sense or self-worth trying to make others receive you when God has not attached them to your destiny.

I especially urge younger men and women not to 'dumb down' by speaking improperly and changing their attire to fit in with those who aren't going anywhere, who have no sense of direction for their lives. Understand that if God has given you vision, He'll put the right people in your life to hold your hand and add value. Expect that some people are not going to like you — not because of what you've done, but simply because you've received revelation about where God wants to take you.

Let me ask you a few questions: Does anybody other than you see where God is trying to take you? Do you have a passion and desire for another level? Do you have financial, educational, and societal goals?

As a precautionary measure — not out of fear, but wisdom — you have to be careful about who you share your God-given dreams with. Those who are closest to you may try to talk you out of your purpose, attempting to lower your sense of self-worth by convincing you that you don't have the ability to get things done. But if God has given you revelation about a goal or an assignment, come Hades or pusillanimous people, no one can stop what God has sanctioned for your life. Likewise, don't allow other people to be so frustrated with you that they talk you out of your dream.

Just as Joseph frustrated his brothers, many of Dr. King's own people were frustrated by him. When he led a protest in Birmingham in 1963, some of the clergy from that town accused him of Marxism and communism, claiming that he broke various laws and city ordinances. In prison, he took a pen and pad and wrote 'Letter from Birmingham Jail', which was included in his famous book, *Why We Can't Wait.* Within those pages, he intimated that people who were supposed to be on his side were, in fact, seemingly operating against him. The specter surrounding these events wreaked havoc on civil rights activities in general and caused disruption between those who had previously been in agreement with Dr. King.

Sometimes your worst enemy is the one who has you on speed dial. Someone close enough to share your secrets and dreams may be the one working to circumvent your progress. Sometimes those who you think should be *for* you are in fact talking and working *against* you.

Joseph's own brothers were threatening to kill him because of his dreams. Now it's sad that while they didn't have dreams themselves, they *did* have a dream for ending his. Isn't it amazing how some people can major in hurting others over minor things? Some people are so insecure with themselves that the only way they can feel better is by pulling others down. Every time you say something positive about someone, there are always the ones who say, "Yeah, but did you hear . . . ?" or, "But I remember in high school . . ." You'll always have people like that in the crowd. When you see that person, you want to respond to them, "Why don't you take your hate-aration somewhere else? Stop worrying about 'but' and ask yourself where you're going with your *own* life." Let them know that you don't have time to spend in negativity, trying to pull down others, when you have a divine assignment and mandate on your own life.

Joseph's brothers said, *"The dreamer is coming. We're going to slay him and cast him into a pit,"* (Genesis 37:19). For years, that was the type of rumbling you heard concerning Dr. King from all parts of the country. It's no secret that people in high places ordered wiretaps and surveillance on the civil rights icon to catch him in a net and do him political, public, and perhaps physical harm. Dr. King had a dream that most people did not understand. You've got to expect hatred and persecution from certain people, but stop seeing them as the enemy. Instead, view the situation as validation that you're on the right track. If everybody likes you and loves you, you're probably going nowhere.

So Joseph's brothers were saying, *"Let's kill him."* Then they threw him into a pit. In Genesis 37:20 (MSG), they say, *"We'll go back and tell our father that some evil beast devoured him. And then we'll see what has become of his dream. We'll kill him and all his fancy dreams. Let's see what happens to them when we kill him."*

Praise Keeps Things from Becoming Fatal

Joseph's brothers were getting ready to kill him, but in Genesis 37:26-27: *"Judah said, 'What profit is it if we slay our brother and conceal his blood? Come, and let us sell him to the Ishmaelites, and let not our hand be upon him; for he is our brother and our flesh.' And his brethren were content."* They were contemplating killing Joseph, their own brother, because of their envy and jealousy. But Judah just wanted to sell him to the Ishmaelites. In effect, he said, "I know y'all want to kill him, but I'm not up for it. Spare him."

In this text, Judah is an actual physical person, but some years after the children of Israel occupied the Promised Land, his descendants formed the land of Judah, now southern Palestine. I like Judah best, not from a personal or geographical standpoint, but based on word study alone. His name actually means 'praise'. What this says to me is that the brothers were ready to kill him, but 'praise' spoke up. 'Praise' says, "You can't kill him because of our family relationship."

Today, you need to thank God that praise can save your life. Have you ever come to church downtrodden, thinking your life was over, when something happened during the worship service that reinvigorated your spirit and your passion? You can testify, "Praise saved my life!"

I'll never forget something that happened to me years ago. I was driving back from Morehouse College in Atlanta to Macon, Georgia, to preach at Beulahland Bible Church (the first church in which I served). As I was driving down the highway, an 18-wheeler truck pulled in front of me. My car went into a tailspin for almost three hundred yards and then stopped safely by the highway median.

When the police arrived and looked at my car, they wondered how I was able to stop safely after the path my car had taken.

What they didn't know was that while the car was spinning, I was shouting, "Jesus!" Yes, I vehemently called on the Lord. Likewise, some of you can testify that there have been times in your lives when you should have been killed, but the praises you sent up saved your life.

If Judah ('praise') had not spoken up, Joseph would have been killed. Instead of killing him, his brothers threw him into a pit. They said, *"Let's see what will become of his dream."* That's tantamount to what happened that fateful day, April 4, 1968, when Dr. King was assassinated. I don't think we'll ever know what actually happened to Dr. Martin Luther King, Jr. Conspiracy theories abound as to why he was killed and by whom. Everything from segregationist infiltration of Dr. King's camp to government intervention has been bandied about. No matter how it happened, or who ultimately pulled the trigger, the fact remains that the purpose of his assassination was to end his dream.

As mentioned earlier, instead of killing Joseph, the brothers threw him into a pit, but then later took him out to sell him to the Ishmaelites. What you've got to realize is that sometimes your pit is the first step toward your favor. Because of where Joseph was going, the pit had to precede his purpose. I'm fully convinced that those yesteryear racists thought that if only they could kill Dr. King, maybe his dreams of social equality, equal access, and school integration would disintegrate.

Thank God that people of all races and nationalities can now go to any public place and enjoy themselves. People of all races can drink out of any water fountain they desire (if they're not afraid of the bacteria that may be swimming in the water). I'm glad many of our cities now have minority leadership. I'm so glad places that were once intrinsically linked to segregation are now places where people of all colors and ethnicities can walk, jog, picnic, and swim together, without fear of retribution. All this is possible, because even if you kill the dreamer you cannot destroy his dream. I thank God that we had a dreamer, and even though that dreamer died, the world is a better place.

The late Maynard Jackson, who I think was responsible for literally and figuratively spreading the wealth, was involved in the city government of Atlanta, Georgia. Thank God for the other minority millionaires, contractors, and businessmen who were blessed because somebody had a dream.

Because Dr. King had a dream, we had Andrew Young, a U.S. ambassador who also ran for Governor of Georgia and served effectively as the Mayor of Atlanta, one of the greatest cities in America. We also had Shirley Franklin, who was Mayor of Atlanta from 2002 to 2010. Now Atlanta is led by Mayor Kasim Reed.

Because we had a dreamer who talked about his dream of social equality to others in his 1963 speech, we're here almost fifty years later, seeing that dream materialize. Martin Luther King, Jr. talked about his dream of his children being judged not by the color of their skin, but by the content of their character. When he gave that speech, the Civil Rights Act had not yet been passed. People were still being lynched in Mississippi, Louisiana, Alabama, and Georgia. In his speech, Dr. King talked about everybody being included, whether Protestant or Catholic, man or woman, or Red, Black, or White. Your orientation and socioeconomic status didn't matter to him, because he believed in justice and equality for all.

While Dr. King was dreaming and prophesying about Blacks and Whites coming together, he had no idea that his speech would have international ramifications. While he was marching, a man from Kenya came to the United States, ended up in Hawaii, and met a woman from Kansas. They became the parents of the first African-American president — Barack Hussein Obama. And forty years after the civil rights dreamer died, this country elected its first non-White president…to the joy of this country and the world.

This is yet another example of how good God is and how anything is possible. To me, this also means that Dr. Martin Luther King, Jr. was not just a dreamer, but a prophet, as well. He wanted justice to flow down like rivers and for righteousness to run down like a stream. Racists thought that when they killed Dr. King, it was the end of the story and that the status quo that had traditionally denied minorities equal access would prevail. Instead, we now have a national holiday to celebrate the birth of America's dreamer.

Again, I ask you: What is your dream? What are your goals for this year? What legacy do you want to leave behind? What specific thing do you believe God has called you to do? The reason the dream lived in Joseph was because God gave the dream to him. Dr. King was able to do what he did because he had a relationship with Jesus Christ. You cannot complete your assignment without a relationship with Jesus.

JUDAH
AS ROLE MODEL

Genesis 38:1-3

Thank God for Judah preventing the other jealous and frustrated brothers from killing Joseph due to Joseph's immaturity and their father's favoritism. But we would do ourselves a disservice if we stopped the lesson of Judah, Joseph's older brother, at chapter 37. There is another part to the story.

This continuation of the story of Judah is specifically helpful, I feel, to both single and married people. Every adult can learn something from Judah, not just in Genesis 37 when he intercedes for his brother, but also in later events that happen in his life.

Because Judah is significant he serves as a model, a paradigm to follow, an example or demonstration for us. In fact, we can glean major principles from Judah's life through the trifocal perspective of him as a single person, as a husband, and as a father. We can then make some applications to our own lives.

After preventing his other brothers from killing Joseph, Judah does four things that both single and married people should be careful not to do.

Don't be Careless or Too Comfortable in Certain Places

Genesis 38:1 says, *"And it came to pass at that time, that Judah went down from his brethren, and turned in to a certain Adullamite, whose name was Hirah."*

For that same verse, the NIV gives us a little more information, *"At that time, Judah left his brothers and went down to stay with a man of Adullam named Hirah."*

The Contemporary English Version says, *"He left the hills and went down to Canaan."*

Judah had been in the hills with his brothers, in a comfortable setting, but he decided to go to the southwest area of Jerusalem. When he got there, he stopped in a Canaanite region. This was particularly important, because what Judah did, in effect, was leave an elevated place and go down from his brethren.

You will know, whether single or married, when you make a weak decision to leave elevated places and go down from them. (I'm not referring to a geographical perspective here. I'm using 'down' as a metaphor for what happens in the spiritual realm.) It's a problem, for instance, when you leave a pure place of worship on Sunday morning and find yourself down in a strip club on Thursday night. When God has elevated you and put you in a stable place, don't ever get too comfortable or careless by setting your mind and affections on worldly things.

The very same situation happened with Jonah. God told him to go to Nineveh to preach to the people there, but because the Ninevites had cruelly mistreated the Israelites, Jonah disobeyed His voice. Instead of going up to Nineveh, not only did he go *down* to Tarshish, he also went *down* in a ship. And then Jonah was thrown *down* into the water and finally *down* into the belly of a great fish.

Some of you have gotten so comfortable and careless in places that are not in alignment and agreement with where you've been called to go by God. The only time you should go *down* is to pick someone up and bring them *up* to where you are.

If you're standing in a pew and someone else is standing on the ground, and you grab their hand, it is much easier for someone who is on the floor to pull you down from that pew than it is for you to pull them up into the pew with you. You've got to know your own sensitivities or vulnerabilities, because what can happen is that you find yourself not doing that which the psalmist mentions in Psalm 1, *"Blessed is the man that walketh not in the counsel of the ungodly, nor standing in the way of sinners, nor sitteth in the seat of the scornful."*

You may think of yourself as very spiritual and holy, but you may find yourself around people and places from which God has already delivered you. As sometimes happens, things are said or done to remind you of the past. You may have heard a song that particularly interested you and got you up on the dance floor before you were saved. Perhaps you will run into someone from your high school days who may have participated with you in less-than-godly behavior. It's during those times that you need to stop walking in the world and start standing on the Word. Even situations that are godly and holy on their face may remind you of things you did in the past. If you're not prayerful, you may eventually find yourself getting caught up in your former, not-so-godly behavior.

Single or married Christian, you have to be careful not to get too comfortable in certain places that take you back to where and what God has delivered you from. Where do you find yourself going all the time?

Now, single women tend to ask me, "Pastor, where is a comfortable and appropriate place for a single person to go?" Even though single men do attend our churches, single women should not come to church just to meet a man. As a matter of fact, in some churches, statistics show that the membership is almost 75% female. So, if you're coming to church to meet a man, you probably will not have much success. Even though many people have been blessed with a 'holy hook-up' in church when God connects them together, that should not be your purpose for coming to worship services.

There are certain appropriate places for Christian women to go to meet men. It's acceptable for a saved woman to go to a basketball or football game, because that's where the men are. It's acceptable if that's your purpose, but most importantly, don't get so caught up in going to certain places to meet someone that you forget to trust in God. You don't want to go to any place if

God is not prioritized, or where there may be a tendency for you to be pulled back into sinful activities. It's okay to meet a man in a grocery store, an airport, or a sports event. You can go to the movies or a football game and not lose your salvation.

On the other hand, don't believe that by staying at home your potential mate will just come to you. It's okay to go to certain places as a single person, but always keep God first. Judah could have stayed in an elevated place, but many things were happening in Adullam that he liked. And so, he left the elevated place and went down.

Don't Commit Yourself to the Wrong Person

This principle applies to both single and married people. Judah went down from the hills to Adullam, the Canaanite region. But the problem with his decision is that the Canaanite region was so messed up that the ungodly inhabitants participated in all types of scandalous practices. There is much written that describes the diabolical nature of the Canaanite era, if you want to research this time period. The people practiced polytheistic worship, child sacrifice, divination, and religious prostitution. In spite of all this, Judah, the one whose name means 'praise', ended up in that problematic place.

Genesis 38:2 says, *"And Judah saw there a daughter of a certain Canaanite."* Now, figuratively speaking, he hadn't gotten a tent, found a job, or joined a church yet. What I'm saying is, he did not establish himself and work toward some level of personal stability. When he got to this place, the first thing he did was find a woman. Now, there's some disagreement in certain theological circles about who this woman was. Some say that her father's name was Shua. Some others say that the girl's name was Shua. Yet the majority of theologians don't even mention the girl's name.

The verse continues, *"And [Judah] took her and went into her."* I'm thinking that a modern-day version of this text would read, "He saw a certain daughter of Shua, and he got to know her," or, "he found out what her educational level was," or, "he found out whether she could make her subjects and verbs agree," or, "he found out what was on her credit report," or, "he found out whether she'd tested positive for HIV/STD."

Instead, the verse says that as soon as Judah saw her, he took her, which lets us know his purpose for going down there in the first place. She's living in this polytheistic region and knows nothing about monotheism and the worship of Jehovah, or the forthcoming Law and the messianic promise given to Abraham. She only knows about the worship of many gods, child sacrifice, divination, religious prostitution, and all kinds of pagan practices. But for Judah, her faith does not matter. If this were happening today, I would say he couldn't care less about her academic prowess, employment status, or whether she could balance a checkbook or clean a house. None of that would have mattered to Judah.

As the children's song verse goes, "You've got to be careful, little eyes, what you see." What I'm saying is that even grownup eyes need to be careful about what they set their sights on. Many of you have gotten into unfruitful relationships simply because you were drawn in by what you saw. Because the woman of your attraction was beautiful and well-endowed, or the man was the epitome of tall, dark, and handsome, you found yourself in a situation that had absolutely nothing to do with the type of person God would have you align yourself with.

Judah, in effect says, "I'm a praiser, but I've still got eyes. And right now my eyes are not on the Lord; they're on this Canaanite girl from Adullam."

Genesis 38:3-5 says, *"She conceived and bare a son; and he called his name Er. And she conceived again . . . and called his name Onan. And she conceived again . . . and called his name Shelah."*

Now, here's the irony: The text never said that Judah made her his wife. Some say that when he 'took her', it means 'as a wife'. But the following verse plainly says that when his firstborn son, Er, became of age, Judah 'took a wife for him'. (Back in those days, marriages were arranged.) So he found a wife for his son Er. But then, why doesn't the text say in verse 2 that Judah took this anonymous, nameless woman as his own wife? Just like during those biblical times, people today seem to be pretty much satisfied with living together without making the union legal.

So now, Judah is 'married' to a woman who shares a totally different faith. Today, a growing segment of young men and women who grew up in evangelical Christian churches are marrying people who don't share their same degree or brand of faith. Subsequently, modern churches are being vilified because they're telling their members not to marry outside of their faith. Some people are asking, "Should it matter whether or not a single person marries somebody who has a different faith? Pastor, if I'm a Muslim and she's a Christian, and we love each other, can we come together and just agree not to have any discussion about our different religious principles?" They argue, "You've got Christians marrying Christians and they still can't get along, even though they both call on the name of Jesus." Others ask me, "Is that what 1 Corinthians means about 'being unequally yoked with unbelievers'?"

I believe that your faith system should be fundamentally the same in terms of the foundation for both of your lives. How are you going to stay committed in a covenant relationship together if you each believe in something totally different? But of course, as the popular '60s song went, "It's your thing/Do what you wanna do". I'm just saying that it's hard to walk together unless you fundamentally agree on who God is and how He would have you live and raise a family (Amos 3:3). Jesus even said, *"A house divided against itself cannot stand." (Mark 3:25)*

Some ask me, "So, Pastor, is it better for me to be a single Christian than to marry a Muslim or an atheist? It's more comforting to me to have a spouse who treats me right, even if we share different faiths." That's a good point, and you have to make your own decision, but I personally believe that you've got to have the same beliefs, faith, context, and foundation.

So getting back to the text, Judah committed himself to someone who didn't share the same faith. As the text showed, he eventually got trapped in a progressively worsening spiral. He had three children by this woman, and then found a wife named Tamar for his oldest son, Er.

Then comes Genesis 38:7: *"And Er, Judah's firstborn, was wicked in the sight of the Lord, and the Lord killed him."* Could it be that his firstborn was wicked because he was raised in a wicked place and his mother came from a lineage of people who were given to wickedness?

This is why you need to be careful who you marry. Single people, before you say 'I do,' make sure you check out your future spouse's entire background. Tell them to take you to their home to meet their parents, grandparents, and cousins, because there's no telling what kind of craziness they have in their lineage. You need to know what kind of spirits, attitudes, and dysfunctions are in their DNA.

Yet some of you marry people without checking them out because you're so in love. But then when your baby is three months old and (hypothetically) starts hissing like a viper, you wonder where that behavior is coming from. It could be something in their DNA. When you marry your spouse, you technically marry your spouse's entire bloodline. And sometimes, dysfunctional behavior skips from generation to generation.

You may wonder why your child is acting crazy at six years old, so you're crying about it, but it's not the child. His abnormal behavior patterns may have been passed down from someone on the father's side of the family who was labeled alcoholic, schizophrenic, or bipolar. That relative was crazy and married someone else who was crazy, and the dysfunction ultimately settled in your child's spirit because you didn't take the time to check out your spouse before you procreated.

You'd better watch out for your children. Sometimes they have a proclivity toward certain physical illnesses because of what's in their DNA and lineage. Such diseases as cancer and hypertension can run through the bloodline. If your parent was a diabetic and had cancer, for example, you may be more susceptible to that. So if that's true in the physical world, it's also true in the spiritual realm.

Don't Get Caught Up in Carnal Pleasures

Er was so wicked that God didn't even allow him to enjoy Tamar. The text says that God killed him. So what happened next?

Judah was trying to be a good parent. His first boy died, so he told his second son, "I'll tell you what. There's something called the levirate marriage ceremony." This comes from the Latin word for 'brother-in-law'. He goes on to explain, "Your older brother Er was killed by God because of his wickedness. Now, Onan, your brother was married to Tamar. What has been permissible and mandated by our society is the law. Since your oldest brother died and his wife didn't have a baby with him, she now becomes your wife. You've got to have a child by her and he won't be legally yours. You will be the surrogate father of this child to perpetuate your brother Er's legacy."

Onan had a responsibility to be Tamar's kinsman-redeemer, a concept mentioned more than once in the Bible. The law was in place — Onan had to marry Tamar. He could have children, but the first one had to be known as his brother's child.

Judah said in Genesis 38:8, *"Go in unto thy brother's wife and marry her, and raise up seed to thy brother."* But notice what Onan did in verse 9: *"But Onan knew that the seed should not be his, and it came to pass, when he went in unto his brother's wife, that he spilled it on the ground, lest that he should give seed to his brother."*

Onan participated in the act, but his heart wasn't in it, and he circumvented the process. Tamar's femininity and womanhood was known and affirmed by her ability to have a child. In biblical times, a woman felt cursed if she could not give birth to a child. But Onan was so selfish that it didn't matter to him if her self-esteem was raised. It didn't matter if their engagement was mutual and productive for both of them. The only thing that seemed to matter to Onan was Onan.

What this says to us today is that we must not get caught up in carnal pleasures. This is a problem with many married couples. You are so busy making sure you're taken care of that you can't or won't engage in a mutual, loving, beneficial relationship. You need to realize that the marriage relationship is not all about you. If you two can't compromise and work on the marriage together, you will have serious relational problems.

This was apparently the case with Onan, though some Bible commentators have suggested that Onan's problem was a much deeper form of selfishness. The purpose of Onan's marriage was to produce a child. If the purpose of your marriage is only pleasure and not the total embodiment of what marriage actually is, then you're on the wrong track.

Don't Lose Focus
When Dealing With Your Passions

Here's what happens next: Judah's first son Er was wicked, and God killed him. Because Onan broke the levirate law and didn't do what he was legally bound to do, God turned around and killed him as well. *"And the thing which he did displeased the Lord: wherefore he slew him also."* (Genesis 38:10)

Judah had a third son. Notice what Judah said to Tamar, his daughter-in-law: "Listen, Tamar, I'll tell you what you're going to do. My first boy Er married you and died. My second boy Onan married you, and he died too. So, I'll tell you what. You go home to your daddy's house and stay there. I've got a third son…Shelah, and I'll send him to you when he gets grown, because I don't want him to die."

Then things got really ugly. Genesis 38:12 says, *"And it came to pass in the process of time that the daughter of Shua, Judah's wife, dies."* So Tamar was single again and living at home as a widow, and Judah's wife died and left him single. The verse continues, *"And Judah was comforted."*

He'd been in mourning, grieving over the loss of his wife. After he finished the grieving process, he went up to Timnath with his friend Hirah for sheepshearing. Hirah urged him to get away for a while.

"And it was told Tamar, saying, 'Behold thy father in law goeth up to Timnath to shear his sheep.' And she put her widow's garments off from her." (Genesis 38:13-14) She'd been wearing widow's clothes, but she heard that her father-in-law was coming to Timnath. So she took off her black garments, covered herself up in a veil, and then sat in an open place. You've got to respect her on the one hand because she was trying to change her situation for the better. The good part is that she realized she'd been a widow too long. Likewise, if you find yourself in a similar situation, at some point when the grief process ends, you've got to stop crying and adorn yourself. Some of you ladies who say you want a godly man to come home to may need to take a good look at yourselves in the mirror. Just because a previous relationship is over, there is no need to let yourself go. You don't have to go around looking frumpy and homely to the point that you don't even make it to the hair salon anymore.

True, everything isn't all about the physical appearance, but men are visual creatures who need something nice to look at. So go ahead and spring for that mani-pedi and buy some makeup. Even if you get it from the corner drugstore, make yourself presentable and attractive when you go out in public. In fact, join a gym and get a personalized workout routine. And if it's a matter of your budget, participate in television exercise. Just do something to enhance yourself physically.

Tamar understood that staying in her house wouldn't change her situation. Now, by this time, Tamar knew that Shelah had grown up. She also remembered that her father-in-law promised her that when he was grown, she would be presented to him in marriage. So she'd been waiting on him to become a man. Now, there's no indication exactly how long she'd been waiting, but it must have been quite a while.

At any rate, her father-in-law came by and saw her sitting in an open place. Genesis 38:15 says, *"Now when Judah saw her, he thought her to be an harlot; because she had covered her face."* Apparently, for him to have considered her a harlot (prostitute), she must have gone over the top in the way she was dressed. Which leads me to this: Ladies, let me just say that you can attract a man without looking like a 'professional'.

"He turned to her by the way and said, 'Go to, I pray thee, let me come in unto thee,'" (Genesis 38:16). Judah was apparently a man of praise who had a problem. Maybe he told himself, "On one side, I'm supposed to praise. But on the other side, I have some untamed passions I have to fight. My wife's dead!" He turned to Tamar, not knowing what she even looked like; it didn't matter to him.

Men, let this be a lesson. If you don't rebuke lust and renew your mind daily with the Word of God, it may become easy to forget what you have at home, or what your station or status in life may be. What is it about some of us who are so worldly, undisciplined, and out of control that we've surrendered everything to God except the libido? And I'm talking about men who have been blessed with beautiful, loving, godly wives. You would think that at this point in his life — when he was probably old enough to have grandkids — that Judah would have matured spiritually. Yet there was something about his lustful nature that kept him undisciplined and unchecked.

Judah didn't even know it was his daughter-in-law with whom he had gotten involved. But it got worse. He was struggling because his wife was dead, and she was struggling because she'd been staying at home too long. So because she was struggling, she put on fancy clothes; because he was struggling, he didn't care what she looked like.

They haggled about what the rendezvous would cost, and Tamar asked for a few goats as payment. Since Judah didn't have goats with him, she ultimately asked for his signet and staff as collateral, and she got them.

The worst thing you can do when you're single, or 'thirsty', is get with another 'thirsty' person. 'Real thirsty' plus 'real thirsty' equals 'real, real thirsty'. 'Thirsty' times 'thirsty' is 'thirsty squared'. You can have someone in your life who, when you're 'thirsty', will offer you their brand of 'water', and you'll drink from that well regardless of how they look or think because you're so caught-up in your lusts and passions. If you've been keeping up with the text, you already know what I'm getting at.

Judah didn't know who she was, but she knew who Judah was. She took the stick. Now, here's the thing: a signet is a ring. You would have thought that she'd view this as promise of a future relationship, but she wasn't interested in the ring. She wanted the goat. A goat? If she was going to ask for something, why didn't she ask for a bull, or a chariot, or even employment within his household? It's a sad commentary on today's world and its changing morals when young ladies have such low self-worth that they'll take anything in exchange for the gift of themselves. I'm just saying . . .

So Judah went in to her, biblically speaking, and she became pregnant. The last part of Genesis 38:16 says, *"What are you going to give me, that you can come on in?"* Paraphrasing, he said, "A goat," and she answered, "Okay, cool!" To her credit, at least she got something. I know that sounds bad, but some men and women have such low self-worth that they allow themselves to be used by anybody, anytime, and they get nothing whatsoever that will benefit them out of the liaison.

Then she groaned about it, "Okay, give me your ring and necklace." He gave it to her and she conceived, (from Genesis 38:18). Then, *"She arose and went away,"* (Genesis 38:19). When she got home, she put her widow clothes back on again. It's as if she was saying, "I'm good for a while."

Judah wanted to be a man of integrity, so he said something like, "I promised I was going to give her a goat. Hey, Hirah, take a goat and give it to her. Get my stick and ring back. Just give her the goat." They went back to that place and tried to find her, but they couldn't. In verse 22, Judah went back and said that he actually had a modicum of integrity. Isn't it interesting how we will try to make it seem as if we have integrity in the middle of jacked-up situations?

In Genesis 38:23, Judah said, "I did what I said I would do. Let her have the ring and the stick because we're going to be shamed." One version says, "We're going to look like fools."

"Three months later it was told to Judah, 'Tamar, your daughter-in-law, is pregnant; she has played the harlot; and behold, she is with child through whoredom " (Genesis 38:24). Isn't that something? The people called her a whore, which was a double standard.

In the same passage, Judah said, *"Bring her forth. We're going to burn her."* So now Judah wanted to follow the Law to the letter by decreeing that Tamar should be killed. Often, the ones who are seemingly more religious among us manage to find a way to condemn everyone else. Be careful about talking about the splinter in someone else's eye while you have a beam hanging out of yours.

So the townsfolk dragged her out of the house and through the streets because of their customs and the Law. They cried, "We're taking you to Judah and then we're going to kill you!"

She said, "I tell you what. Before you kill me, take him this stick and ring. Whoever owns these things is the father of my child."

So Judah, who was getting ready to kill her, acknowledged the items and ended up admitting, *"She has been more righteous than I,"* (Genesis 38:26). Yet he didn't tell them all his business; he didn't tell them what he did with her. He just said that he was supposed to have betrothed her to his third son. He wanted the townspeople to leave Tamar alone, and he himself didn't want to discuss it further. The next verse said that he 'knew her no more', which was a good thing.

But Tamar ended up with twin sons fathered by Judah. When it came time for her to give birth, one of them put his arm out first and the midwife tied a scarlet string around his hand, signifying that he was the firstborn. Then the second one came out. The firstborn was named Pharez, and the second son was named Zarah. Yet even though Pharez actually came out first, Zarah's hand was the one that had stuck out.

What happened here? Judah made mistakes as a single man by going to Canaan in the first place. Then he made another mistake by marrying the wrong woman. Because Judah didn't check his wife out first, his firstborn son Er grew up spiritually challenged because he was in a crazy environment. Then his second son Onan was spiritually challenged as well.

Parents, if you have three children and the first two appear rather dysfunctional, stop walking in denial by telling yourselves you have no idea where that foolishness exhibited by your children is coming from. Children are a reflection of their environment and lineage, and sometimes you reap in your children what you sowed in your own life.

Anyway, Onan and Er died. Tamar and Judah, both single again, hooked up. They were caught up in a situation that they made a mess of because they didn't handle the single life properly. They ended up with no love or commitment, but nonetheless had two babies in the process. In your own life, you may have transgressed only one time, but you don't need me to tell you, that may be all that it takes.

What do you do if you've messed up as a single? What if you've married somebody to try to clean up the situation your actions wrought? The good thing about Judah is that he didn't marry Tamar just because she was pregnant. This is how gracious God is. Because Judah didn't kill her, and he cut off the desire of the townspeople to kill her, God did something for him. Tamar, the one who was so messed up that she couldn't handle her passions, ended up in the lineage of Jesus Christ. According to Matthew 1:3, baby Pharez is connected to David and became an ancestor of Mary and Joseph, the parents of Jesus. Even though this baby was born in the middle of a messed-up situation, God was so awesome and gracious that He brought something positive out of it.

I don't care how bad your life has been. Perhaps like Onan, Judah, and others, you can admit that before and maybe even after you turned your life over to Christ that you made some wrong decisions. You associated with the wrong people and may be experiencing repercussions to this very day. But here's the good news: You can go to the Lord and say, "God, I can't change what happened yesterday, but You can change me now for the future. This I pray in Jesus' name." He will turn things around for you. Even with children who you didn't want at the time because they reminded you of a relationship that wasn't of God, the Lord has a way of using you and your children to bring something glorious out of a less than glorious situation.

GOOD IDEA VERSUS GOD IDEA

Genesis 39:1-2

You need to discern the difference between a good idea and a God-inspired dream. Many of us have visions or dreams, but the challenge is this: Are we sure of the giver? Are we certain of the source and origin of that dream?

Hear me out before you wrinkle your nose at what follows. I think that some of us have been negatively impacted by our parents' and grandparents' desire for us to live a life that was better than our ancestors' lives. They made a concerted effort to foster positive self-awareness, self-image, and self-esteem by encouraging us to do and be anything we wanted. Why? Because they did not want us living lives of limitation the way they perhaps lived. They didn't want us to think a lack of certain professional or financial opportunities meant we could not do what others, perhaps more fortunate, had the opportunity to accomplish.

Now, here's where I'm going with this: I'm inspired and encouraged by the movie *Red Tails* because it shows all of us, regardless of race or ethnicity, that you can accomplish whatever you set out to do.

But the negative side of that coin is that so many of us have looked within ourselves to determine what we want to do, without the benefit of conferring with or hearing from God. Because we've read in the Bible that God will give us the desires of our hearts if we delight ourselves in Him, we sometimes omit the other side of the equation. There is a difference between God giving us the desires of our hearts, passions, and principles, and discovering the purpose for which we've been created. We cannot fathom, ascertain, or dictate the reasons for our creation because we did not create ourselves. Since we're not the givers of life, we have to be in touch with the One who gave us life and honestly say to Him, "You are the manufacturer of life. Can You clearly reveal to me the reasons why You allow me to exist?"

Then He'll explain to you your individual purpose, the plan for your life that was decided prenatally, just as He told Jeremiah, *"Before I formed you I knew you. I sanctified you and I had already ordained you to be a prophet to the nations."* (Jeremiah 1:5)

You were born with a purpose, and God will grant you the desires of your heart if you delight yourself in Him. But even if you don't delight in Him, that does not negate or change the reason you were created. So first and foremost, before you get into the distinctive nuances of your particular dream, ask yourself if you can be sure that your dream is in alignment and agreement with what you heard in your spirit as the reason God created you. If not, you're going to be diametrically opposed to the very reasons for your existence.

Joseph had been given a dream that was not of his own making. His dream was not based on human ambition because he had no idea what he was going to do. He knew he was created to fill some type of ruling capacity, but the specifics had not yet been revealed. He saw his brothers and father as the stars and the moon bowing down to him, but the actual interpretation and manifestation of his dream had not yet been given to him.

And so Joseph's dream appears to have gotten him into some trouble. Even though his life is actualized by this dream, this chapter goes on and on without reference to the dream that is to fuel him. Nor is the purpose for which he was born materially evident at this point. He has to, in effect, operate outside the dream. Our challenge today is if we don't know how to operate in a godly way outside the dream, we'll never be fully functional within the context of the dream.

Entire sections of Genesis are what I like to refer to as 'preparatory passages' of evolution, development, and maturation. The Joseph we see in the beginning of this text is not the same person we see toward the end of the chapter. Early on, Joseph, in my view, is not a likeable character, in part because he's not actually walking toward the lofty nature of what he has dreamed. When Joseph received his dreams about the sheaves and the sun, moon, and stars, he promptly told his brothers about them. He was basically telling them, "I want you to know that I'm going to be all that and a bag of chips." He talked like that within the context of his dream.

There are instances in Joseph's life that can certainly be viewed from a positive perspective, in that we learn what we're supposed to do while we're living apart from the dream God has planted within. Indeed, the latter chapters serve as prerequisites, the next steps to getting what God has ordained. If you believe that God has called you to accomplish something special, take a look at Joseph and learn the following life principles for operating outside of the dream while you wait for manifestation.

Develop a New Form of Communication

Instead of killing Joseph, his brothers sold him to a band of Ishmaelites, who, in turn, sold him to be a slave for Potiphar, the captain of the guard in Pharaoh's court.

"And the Lord was with Joseph, and he was a prosperous man." Although he was enslaved and dominated on the lower rung of the socioeconomic ladder by another ruling ethnic group in Egypt, Joseph was still prosperous and blessed in Egypt.

The Message Bible renders it a little differently: *"And it turned out that God was with Joseph, and things went very well for him. Joseph ended up living in the home of his Egyptian master."* The NIV says, *"Joseph was very successful."* The King James Version says, *"He was prosperous."*

But Joseph has not yet said a word. When all he had was a dream, Joseph ran his mouth about his brothers' sheaves and the sun and moon and stars bowing down to him. And all the while he was doing what we refer to today as talking trash — still living at home and still broke. Yet he ran his mouth about the possibilities life held for him.

But now, this same Joseph who ran his mouth when he had nothing has so far not said a word. In this new chapter of his life, when he is anointed, appointed, and aware, Joseph's success is not based on what he has said. Which brings me to this: You need a new form of communication when God has given you a dream or assignment. In other words, you don't have to talk about it. All you have to do is show up and let the favor and prosperity of God do your speaking for you.

The problem with many of us is that we're always running our mouths about what we know, how smart and gifted and wonderful and beautiful we are, all the people we've helped, everything we've experienced, and all the accolades we've received for our accomplishments. Many of us brag about having more degrees than a thermometer, or of being the first ones in our families to do such and such.

The best thing you can do is shut your mouth and let the glory on your life speak for you! If the dream is on your life, you don't even have to open your mouth. Let God speak for you. Sometimes all you have to do is show up. You'll discover that God has worked behind the scenes and your success will speak for you.

This is the difference between people who just have money and wealthy people with money and class. A problem with many of us, particularly those of us who are middle-class, is that we want our economic status to speak for us. So you make a six-figure income, buy a house in a nice neighborhood, and then want your ostentation to speak for you. You want to let others know that you have arrived. And so, what happens is that you start thinking that cars, clothes, cash, homes, and other creature comforts are the things you have to show others in order to prove how successful you are.

So the Mercedes Benz you drive has 24-inch chrome wheels on it. You're technically broke but feel as if you have to buy thousand-dollar hand-sewn suits to show that you can have the best your wallet can buy. And here you are, two paychecks away from being evicted, yet all that material stuff is speaking for you, or so you think.

Wealthy folks understand the way it should be done. They can drive a used subcompact because their material possessions don't define them. One of the greatest deliverances you can ever get is when you stop buying clothes you can't afford to impress the people who don't even like you. I promise, they're talking about you regardless of what you're wearing. Let your success speak for you. Stop bragging by announcing your titles. Then when folks look at you, they can truly understand you. It's a new form of communication.

What kind of communication do you use at work? Don't be on the job undermining coworkers and being cutthroat. Just have the right attitude and let your work ethic promote you.

Joseph was not prosperous in the earlier chapters. Maybe it's because he was talking too much. Once he became quiet, God began speaking for him. Joseph was not even operating in the context of his dream since he was enslaved in Egypt, but he had chosen to use a new form of communication.

Delight in the Father's Affirmation

"And his master saw that the Lord was with him and that the Lord made all that he did to prosper in his hand. And Joseph found grace in Potiphar's sight, and he served him; and he made him overseer over his house, and all that he had he put into his hand."
(Genesis 39:3-4)

Joseph was concerned about his dreams of his brothers' sheaves and the sun, moon, and stars bowing down to him in obeisance.

"Joseph found favor in his sight, and he served him."
(Genesis 39:4)

Here, there's no mention of the dreams; instead, the one who wanted to be bowed down to earlier was serving the lord of the manor. Potiphar saw that the Lord was with Joseph, so he made him the overseer of his entire household. But, why? Even though God had affirmed him in Potiphar's eyes, Joseph was no longer stuck on his dreams; in fact, he was paying homage to Potiphar.

There are those of you who want to be at the top of your game in order to operate in your dream. But until you figuratively stop by Potiphar's house and serve someone else, you will not be truly successful in the Lord's eyes. Many want to be served, but the dream will not manifest unless you take off your Sunday best, don your overalls, and ask God how you can be a blessing to someone else. God will then affirm you as a result of your willingness and ability to serve others.

What you do right now in this season is a direct seed that one day is going to germinate. So, if you're not sowing seeds now, don't look for a harvest later. There are those of you who tend to be a thorn in your supervisor's side because you think you're smarter, or can do the job better, or have more experience or education than your manager does. Even though all of that may be true, the grudging way you're serving right now is what your supervisor will remember. When your turn comes up and you're in a position to be promoted, guess what's going to happen? You're going to end up reaping the same thing you're sowing. So be careful of the seeds you sow right now.

Why does Genesis 37 never say that the Lord was with Joseph, or that his father and brothers saw that God was with him? He was too busy 'uncovering his brothers' nakedness' and not busy enough serving his siblings or his father.

But Potiphar saw something in Joseph that even his fathers and siblings did not see. If his brothers had seen God's hand on him, they would never have sold him, or ever thought about killing him. But because he was so stuck on the dream and not on the process, they wanted to get rid of him.

We're all in a maturation process of some sort. If you're operating out of the wrong season, nothing will work for you. For some of you, now is not the season for buying a new car just because your neighbor just did. Please stop trying to be affirmed by others and consider, just for a moment, that you may be in a serving season right now. Tell yourself this for encouragement, "I'm not jealous of what they have. I thank God for their new car (or house, or flat-screen), because I know when God blesses my neighbor, He's blessing the neighborhood. I'm in a season of sacrifice and serving, and this is where I'll operate until it's time to go to the next level."

And here's something else: You don't know what your neighbor or coworker or cousin has to go through trying to hold on to what they have. You just have to pray, "God, I'm going to let You affirm me while I'm serving, in Jesus' name."

And bear in mind that this may very well be outside of the dream — but that's okay. Don't be so focused on the future that you can't delight in the Father's affirmation right now.

Resolve to Remain Faithful

"It came to pass from the time that Potiphar made Joseph the overseer of his house and over all that he had, the Lord blessed the Egyptian's house," (Genesis 39:5). Potiphar's house was blessed, not because of Potiphar, but because he had the right person in his camp.

You'd better be careful about who you let into your house and who you have around you. Some people, even Christian folks, are so drama-filled, deceitful, and messy that their spirit of messiness may rub off on you. Conversely, you can be blessed simply because you're connected to the right person.

Two years ago. I had the opportunity to visit the White House with my family and some friends from my family church back home. We got the opportunity to minister to some of the people who worked in the United States Secret Service. At the gate, they gave us badges that allowed us unrestricted access. Visitors on the normal tours were only allowed to go into certain areas, but our access was expanded. However, somewhere along the way, I got disconnected from my badge.

As I was trying to enter an area in the West Wing, the Secret Service stopped me, saying that I didn't have proper access to that part of the White House. I said, "Well, I'm a guest of Mr. So-and-So, who works for the president. I've been ministering to him and all the people who work with him."

I was told to hold on while my name was checked against the list. Once the list was checked and they verified my name and confirmed my connection with someone who worked directly for the president, I was in like Flynn. Let me tell you, benefits, flexibilities, and access were immediately bestowed upon me. Not because of who I was, but because of who I was connected with.

In the same way, when you are connected to God and the right people, there will be instances when all you have to do is show up and the door will just open. It's not because you're wonderful and fabulous, but is a direct result of who you're connected with in your inner circle.

So Potiphar's house was blessed because Joseph was there: *"And the Lord blessed the Egyptian's house for Joseph's sake, and the blessing of the Lord was upon all that he had in the house, and in the field. And he left all that he had in Joseph's hand; and he knew not ought he had, save the bread which he did not eat. And Joseph was a goodly person, and well favoured."* (Genesis 39:5-6)

This is how the Message Bible puts it: *"[Even after the blessing] all Potiphar had to concern himself with was eating three meals a day."*

Joseph managed Potiphar's entire household, including his money, bills, sheep, and servants. Potiphar had placed so much trust in Joseph that he only had to do three things every day — eat breakfast, lunch, and dinner. Joseph ran everything else in his household.

Yet even after Joseph was elevated, he obviously didn't allow the prosperity of God to change his level of faithfulness. But be mindful of this: God cannot and will not bless some of you because He knows that if He prospers you, He's going to lose you. So, in order to keep you talking to Him, God is no doubt saying, "I'm going to keep you broke because it's the only thing that keeps you praying."

People say that money doesn't change you, but that's not true. Now, money may not make you better; it just magnifies what's already there. This means that if somebody has a crack cocaine problem and they get some money, they're just going to buy more crack cocaine. But money *can* make a difference in your life. If you don't believe that, look at photos of certain celebrities *before* their wallets became fat.

There are those who reach a certain socioeconomic level and suddenly believe that others are beneath them. Picture being around someone who acts as if they're smelling something foul in the air. Imagine that same person during church fellowship who used to offer their entire hand in friendship, but now only presents three fingers for you to grab onto. And what about those who use to 'tear the church up' with loud, joyful praise of God, who, now that their bank accounts are swollen, have become more subdued during worship?

The true sign of your maturity and spirituality involves your ability to treat people in the same kind and considerate manner you always have. When you do this, you'll still have the same praise and worship style, the same personality, and the same humility. You'll still have the same personality driving a Mercedes Benz as you did while riding public transportation. You're the type of person God is looking to abundantly bless.

So don't get to a certain level and stop being faithful and committed. Joseph could have changed when he became prosperous, but he didn't. When you achieve your dream, will you change? When you get to where God wants you to be, will you be different in a worse way, or will you still be faithful? Even after all the promotions he received, Joseph was still so faithful that Potiphar trusted him completely and elevated him beyond measure.

Also, you need to start looking at your life to determine if the right people are in it. Hypothetically, it may be that some of you single females once had great credit scores, money in the bank, and peace and tranquility. But then you met some man, let your guard down, and allowed Mr. Wrong into your life. After all that, your credit score has plummeted, your checking account is overdrawn, and you're in emotional turmoil. Warning bells should have gone off in your head to alert you to the fact that you were about to let the wrong person into your life.

Similarly, some of you men have had good women in your lives, and you were paying your child support and bills on time and seeing your kids regularly. But now you've dropped the good one because you've set your sights on this new woman whom you assumed had more to offer. The result may well be that now you're behind on child support, you're not seeing your children, and everything in your life is in disarray. It could be that what you have invited into your scope and sphere is not of God.

You need to add someone tantamount to a Joseph — or, for you men, a Josephina — into your life. When they're around, your life is lifted up to the next level. On the other hand, you don't need someone who will take you backward. You've got to reach the point where you realize that you can do bad all by yourself. You don't need liabilities, only assets. You've got enough trouble trying to walk in holiness; you don't want someone in your life who takes you back to what God has delivered you from. The question you need to ask yourself is this: Have I gone to the next level since this person has been in my life? Hopefully, that level is upward.

Joseph got the blessing, and Potiphar's entire household was blessed because of him. Joseph was aware that he was walking toward his dream, but he never changed. He was consistent. I submit to you that success was happening in Joseph's life despite the fact that he was not focusing on his dream. He was not ready for the dream in chapter 37, so God took him through a maturation process.

Discipline Your Flesh to Fight Temptation

Potiphar's house was blessed because Joseph was there. All of Potiphar's money, assets, and land were overseen by Joseph. He was a slave, but now he was running the entire house so well that Potiphar didn't even have to worry about his business affairs.

"And Joseph was a strikingly handsome man," (Genesis 39:6). So not only was Joseph favored of God and managing all the accounts in Potiphar's house as a prosperous businessman, he was also 'easy on the eyes'. It appears Joseph was headed for a serious *spiritual challenge.*

"And it came to pass after these things, that his master's wife cast her eyes upon Joseph," (Genesis 39:7). Potiphar's wife looked on this blessed, spiritual, business-savvy, strikingly handsome man and determined that in some way, form, or fashion, she had to have him.

Brothers and sisters in Christ, let this be a lesson for you. I'm not condoning Potiphar's wife's attitude, but sometimes you can be so busy taking care of everything else that maybe you've forgotten your responsibilities at home, and you begin to neglect what you've been blessed with. Husbands, I know you want to play golf and make more money to send the kids to school, but you've still got responsibilities at home. Wives, I know you're busy, but you've got…a headache. Remember, that's what they make aspirin and other pain relievers for.

I don't know what Potiphar's wife's problem was, but I surmise that it was demonic. Joseph is godly, but the text never says that about Potiphar or his wife.

She was so moved and smitten with Joseph, but the Bible says, "He refused." Joseph was spiritually and physically a strong man, an awesome presence in his master's house. (And you know that Potiphar must have had a pretty wife.

Now the text doesn't say that; I'm just making an assumption based on his status.)

He had enough sense to refuse. He said, *"There's no one greater in this house than me. He's not kept anything back from me but you. You're his wife. I can't do this great wickedness and sin against God. It's not against Potiphar. My issue is with God."* (Genesis 39:8-9)

"And it came to pass, as she spake to Joseph day by day . . ." (Genesis 39:8-9). So this flirtation didn't just happen that one time. Can you imagine her adorning herself and then walking by Joseph every day? This temptation didn't come to Joseph just one time and then he was done with it. No, day by day this same persistent temptation came to him. But the text tells us that he would not 'hearken to her voice'.

"And it came to pass that Joseph went into the house to do his business, and there was none of the men of the house there within." (Genesis 39:11) It was just Joseph and his master's wife alone in the house. Verse 12 says, *"she caught him by his clothes."* She was tired of talking. She grabbed him by his clothes and snatched them off. But here's what impresses me about Joseph: Even though he had access to his master's wife and undoubtedly could have gotten away with whatever she had planned for him, this time Joseph understood that desperate situations require desperate and immediate actions. So what did he do? He fled the house and escaped her clutches.

You've got to arrive at that place in your life where you can immediately leave a tempting situation. For instance . . . men, hear me out. If while at work you're walking toward the water cooler and happen upon a coworker dressed provocatively, avert your eyes and keep walking. Why? James 4:7 says, *"Resist the devil, and he will flee from you."* Don't trust yourself in situations when you know you're weak. There are some people you can't talk to. There are some phone calls you just can't take.

Why did Joseph resist the temptation? Probably because he told himself, "If it weren't for God, I would have been killed in the pit. I've got to be faithful to Him for sparing my life. It was God who kept me in Potiphar's house. It was God who gave me everything I've got. Because of that, I've got to be faithful. God has given me a dream, and if I allow my flesh to get in the way of it, I may abort the things He has planned for me. I can't put myself in situations that I know will make me disobey and disrespect God."

Men, stop making excuses such as, "I'm just a man." No, you're not just a man. You're a man of God who's been saved by the blood of Christ. You've been sanctified. There is no temptation given to man from which God won't provide a way of escape. You can look at a woman and say she's pretty, but don't forget your purpose and how God has delivered you.

Too many of us make too many excuses. So, does God have the power to save you but not keep you? Do you mean to tell me that God does not give you the ability to walk away?

Are you that egotistical fellow who just has to run after every woman who gives you that 'come hither' look?

Some things you've got to shun. Make declarations such as these to fortify your spiritual resolve:

- I can't do illegal drugs.

- I can't steal money from my job, my family, my friends, etc.

- I'm not going to drink alcohol to excess.

- I am not going to allow any type of lust to overtake me.

Remember, it's in Him that you move, live, and are. If it had not been for the Lord on your side, where would you be? Understand that you've got to be obedient and faithful, and He'll give you the good of the land. Ask God to help you have more than charisma. Ask God to give you the character to say no, even when something presented before you looks good and tempting.

OCCUPY THE DREAM

Genesis 40:4-8

T here's been much in the news this year about the Occupy movements, which began as international protests of economic and social inequality. These people came on the scene to protest what they felt was social injustice and financial disenfranchisement. In the beginning, it seemed to be a loose-knit organization with no specific goals in mind. Since that time, it's expanded and is now called the Occupy the Dream Movement, which closely resembles the earlier Civil Rights Movement sparked by Dr. King's dream of equality and opportunity for all.

It may be that occupying the dream includes those to whom the dream wasn't initially given. But just who is expected to help individuals occupy? Is this movement only directed toward Wall Street? Is this movement only directed toward those would-be "oppressors"? Who are the overseers of this Occupy movement? What are the inherent challenges?

While collectively you may be excited about the possibility of justice coming down like waters and righteousness like a mighty stream, it's important to understand that sometimes your responsibility to break through is not in the hands of others. Simply put, you cannot just sit back and let others do for you what God has assigned you to do for yourself.

Genesis is partly about Joseph, who was eventually able to occupy his dream. Joseph was given a dream by God early on, yet by the time Genesis wound down, his dream still had not materialized.

It's one thing to have a dream; it's another to actually occupy that dream. It's one thing to be motivated by a dream, but it's another thing to see the manifestation of that dream. Toward the end of the chapter, Joseph goes from being motivated by a dream to seeing it manifested. He literally occupies the dream that God has given him.

Similarly, from an individual perspective to a corporate one, God has given us the ability to do what Joseph did. We should not merely wait for others to do things for us in our lives, but rather engage ourselves in a process of personal development and responsibility to walk in that which God has ordained for us.

Even though manifestation of his dream was imminent, there were things Joseph had to do to take full possession. God's purpose for you, such as starting a new business or going back to school, will not happen by itself. In order to occupy the dream, there are steps in a process that you have to take before you see the manifestation of what God has shown you.

Develop a Concern for Others

When Joseph received his dream, he was only concerned with sheaves and the sun, moon, and stars bowing down to him. It appears he was self-aggrandizing. He felt as if everything was about him. Because of his lack of maturity, Joseph had a tough row to hoe. Eventually, he came across a desperate housewife who falsely accused him of sexual impropriety; he was thrown in prison by Potiphar, his employer.

While Joseph was in prison, God continued to bless him. In the meantime, Pharaoh became upset with two of his employees — a butler and a baker — and threw them in prison with Joseph. When he was in prison, Joseph was made the overseer. What you can take away from this is that sometimes, when the blessing is on you, it doesn't matter where you go; God will bless you wherever your feet shall tread.

"And it came to pass that on the same night, both the butler and the baker had a dream. Joseph looked upon them; and, behold, they were sad," (Genesis 40:5-6). It appears that Joseph had developed concern for someone else.

When your mind has you believing it's all about you, you will never be able to occupy the dream that God has given to you. At the end of the day, your dream is not ultimately about you. If God can't be glorified and people can't be edified through what God has given you, it's not a God-inspired dream. It's merely a wish, or an item on your personal agenda.

Yet God is able to get a blessing *to* the people that He's able to get a blessing *through.* When you achieve your dream, how will you use it to bring someone else to a higher level? Whether it's your family, friends, or people in general, do you have a concern for others, or is it all about you?

Cultivate Your God-Given Potential.

In Bible days, many believed that every dream they had was a word from God. They actually thought He was always trying to speak something into their lives. He is, but not everything He tells you is something you're supposed to share with others. Now, the butler and the baker both had significant but problematic dreams, and they ended up perplexed.

Joseph agreed to interpret the dreams for them, which was a first for a man who, in the beginning, was only concerned about himself. This was a different Joseph. God placed potential within him. There are skills he had to develop because he needed them to propel him to his destiny.

Not operating in the midst of your manifestation or not living the dream you believe God placed in your heart can be upsetting. Perhaps you're not there yet because skills have to be cultivated, lessons have to be learned, and your dull edges need sharpening. If you get to the point of manifestation and you don't possess the skills, discernment, and spiritual gifts needed, you may short-circuit the dream because you're not prepared.

Think of it like taking a cake out of the oven before its time. Many a cook has ruined their cake by pulling it out of the oven too soon. Good thing someone finally figured out that you should stick a toothpick in the middle to see if it's done.

You may be frustrated because you look good on the outside but aren't making progress. But remember, God knows if there are things going on inside you that aren't stable yet. Let Him keep you in a place of waiting in order to develop all your gifts. You may think you're ready, but if you're not rooted and grounded, you'll mess up the blessings of God. The Lord wants you to cultivate your potential on your way to realizing your dream.

Pray this is Jesus' name: "God, don't send me anywhere before I'm ready. If You don't think I'm ready or equipped, keep me in the oven long enough. God, keep sharpening me and working on me so that when I get there, I can maintain that next level."

You can possibly destroy a lifetime of blessings because you tried on your own to accomplish the dream too soon. You must take heed to develop your God-given potential by learning how to pray for your neighbor, by speaking to people who don't like you, by forgiving, and by growing spiritually. It's good that you have a dream, but He wants you to be able to multi-task. And even though Joseph had never interpreted anyone else's dream before, he understood that God had given him that gift. Ask yourself: What gifts do I have that I haven't developed yet?

Don't Get Comfortable in the Wrong Places

Both the butler and the baker had dreams, and Joseph believed that God was going to give him the ability to interpret them. Even though Joseph's own dream was yet to be interpreted and its meaning made clear, he was more concerned with interpreting the dreams of others and helping them understand their true meaning.

The butler told Joseph his dream, *"There were three branches on a vine that were budding and blossoming. Grapes were coming forth. Pharaoh's cup was in my hand, and I took the grapes and pressed them into the cup."*

Joseph replied, *"What the dream means is this: The three branches represent three days. In three days you will be restored to your position that you lost when you were thrown into jail."*

The baker said, *"Tell me the meaning of my dream. I had three white baskets on my head, filled with bread for Pharaoh to eat. But birds came and ate the bread out of the baskets."* Let's just say Joseph told him that the dream had nothing to do with restoration.

He said to the butler, *"Yet within three days shall Pharaoh lift up thine head, and restore thee unto thy place: and thou shalt deliver Pharaoh's cup into his hand, after the former manner when thou wast his butler. But think on me when it shall be well with thee. Show me kindness, I pray thee, unto me, and make mention of me unto Pharaoh, and bring me out of this house."* (Genesis 40:13-14)

In other words, "Listen, when you get back to being the bartender, do me a favor. When you're back in Pharaoh's presence, bring up my name. Let him know I was stolen out of the land of the Hebrews. They put me here in the dungeon, and I haven't done anything wrong."

Now, the Bible says that Joseph was blessed while he was in prison. *"But the Lord was with Joseph and showed him mercy, and gave him favor in the sight of the keeper of the prison. And the keeper of the prison committed to Joseph's hand all the prisoners. The keeper of the prison looked not to any thing that was under his hand."* (Genesis 39:21-23) In other words, he trusted Joseph. Everything he did in jail, *". . . the Lord made it to prosper."*

Do you think that maybe, if you were in his shoes, you would have gotten comfortable? Do you think that you would have regarded yourself with more self-esteem than you should? What Joseph saw in his dream did not line up with where he was at that point in time. When what God has shown you does not look like where you are right now, make sure not to get too comfortable in that place, because it's not the sum total of all that He has for you.

If you know by the stripes of Jesus that you are, were, and will be healed, but the doctor shows you a spot on the X-ray, don't say, "I'm going to die." Just say, "Doc, I understand the reality, but what you're saying doesn't look like or sound like what God's showing me. I'm not going to get too comfortable with your diagnosis."

Start believing that when God shows you something, you've got to keep trusting in what He has shown you until where and what you are resembles where and what He said you're going to be. Never settle for less when God has more.

Personally, I want everything God has assigned to me. People say, "You should be satisfied with what you have. Why don't you slow down? You're moving too fast. Just be good with where you are." Now, I'm good with where I am. No matter what state I'm in, I've learned to be content there. Even if all I have to eat are crackers, potted meat, and bologna, I'm going to be satisfied.

But why be satisfied with vienna sausages when God wants to give me filet mignon and chateaubriand steak? Don't get too comfortable because you're making six figures on your job, especially when God has shown you in your vision that He's got a fantastic business idea for you. Stop being satisfied in the proverbial prison when the dream is designed to take you to the palace. Joseph was probably saying to himself, "I know I've got a good job, being in charge of everything in this jail. But this isn't lining up with that amazing dream I had so many years ago."

There's an irony here. The butler and baker were both dreamers. It's interesting that before Joseph could occupy his dream, he had to be around others who were dreamers as well.

You will never occupy your dream if you choose to surround yourself with slackers. God may be trying to show you that you've got to be around other people who are dreamers before you can achieve your own dream. If you're around people who are takers, they'll just suck the life out of you. Instead, you've got to be around like-minded people who believe God has a better day with more in store.

Your prayer in Jesus' name should be, "God, surround me with other dreamers who can encourage me when I don't believe in my own dream anymore."

Don't Let Your Associations Prevent You From Being Positive

After three days, the butler was restored to his former position with the Pharaoh. *"The king restored the chief butler to his butlership again and he gave the cup into Pharaoh's hand,"* (Genesis 40:21). So the butler got his job back.

Remember that Joseph, who had interpreted his dream, said, "When you're delivered, remember who told you the interpretation of your dream."

"Yet did not the chief butler remember Joseph, but forgot him." (Genesis 40:23)

Isn't it sad when some of the people you helped in the past are the same ones who forget you? Don't ever burn a bridge by forgetting the people who helped you get to where you are. Young people today seem to have forgotten their ancestors who sacrificed so they could have a good life. When people have blessed you, you shouldn't forget about them.

Joseph set a good example for us to follow. He could have been royally angry at the butler. If given the chance, he could have forcefully reminded the butler that had he not intervened and interpreted, the butler would not be enjoying his newfound freedom. Yet Joseph, who had become a man of integrity, did not allow the butler's forgetfulness to change him into someone bitter and vengeful.

So, where are we? Oh, yeah, the butler returned to his previous status.

Two years later, Pharaoh had a dream that no one in his house could interpret. *"Then spake the chief butler unto Pharaoh, saying, 'I do remember my faults this day,' "* (Genesis 41:19). In other words, "Hey, boss, I forgot to tell you this. About two years ago I got thrown in jail and Joseph interpreted my dream."

Joseph was brought out of the prison that very day. What this passage suggests is that even if the seeds you have sown take a while to produce, if you've been faithful, everything will work out just fine. It's impossible to sow good seeds in the soil of God and not reap a harvest. Galatians 6:9 says, *"Don't be weary in well-doing, for in due season you will reap if you faint not."* Somebody, somewhere will remember.

Joseph told the Pharaoh, "The dream you had about seven fat cows and seven lean ones means that you'll have seven years of prosperity followed by seven years of famine. You'll have some good years followed by some rough years. But King, while the good years are happening, prepare for the famine. While it's feast time, don't spend everything."

"And Pharaoh said unto his servants, 'Can we find such a one as this, a man in whom the Spirit of God is?'" (Genesis 41:38). It's as if he said, "I see God in this one. You know what, boys? Joseph has been in jail, but the good news is, jail is not in him."

When a person is surrounded by negativity, they will often allow that negativity to make them bitter. But Joseph didn't allow his circumstances to change the God in him. As a result, he got a promotion, a wife, work, and wealth. He was thirty when he became the second most powerful man in all of Egypt. It took thirteen years for Joseph to be moved from the motivation to the manifestation of his dream.

Because he didn't sin with Potiphar's wife, God blessed Joseph with a wife of his own and two sons. *"And unto Joseph were born two sons before the years of famine came."* (Genesis 41:50)

I can hear Joseph saying, "You know what? When I look at my life, now I can occupy the dream. I've got two sons.

I'm going to name my first son 'Manasseh', which means 'I'm going to forget all the mess that I went through to get to where I am now.' "

Despite all the pain caused him by the Enemy, he wanted to forget all those things and press on toward the mark. He named his second son Ephraim, which means 'double prosperity'. He said, "For everything I gave up, He's going to give me double for my trouble, because I was able to have integrity with my dream."

Whatever God has assigned for your life, hold on to that dream. Forget all the situations you endured that were personally negative to the point of being devastating. I've got good news for you. If God has revealed it to you, your time and new season will come, according to His will.

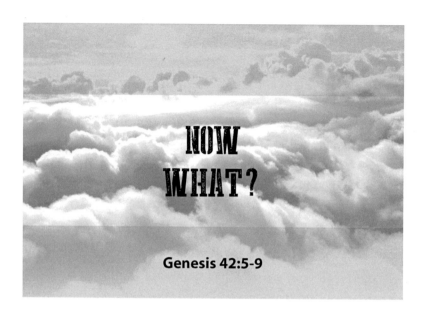

NOW WHAT?

Genesis 42:5-9

Success can kill your dream.

The purpose in this chapter is not to discuss the nuances, negativities, or challenges that may impact the life of someone living their dream. No matter who they are, no one is exempt from life's trials and tribulations.

You have no doubt heard and read about celebrities who were so talented, gifted and successful, who died shockingly due to drug overdose, suicide, or even homicide. The ultimate challenge for when you begin to walk in your dream, and are inarguably on the way to success, is how you are going to handle things when your dream finally comes true.

When you're on the rise, trying to reach your individual goals, it's not about the struggle, the sacrifice, or the sweat, blood, and tears you've put into seeing the manifestation of those dreams. Instead, the greatest dilemma can arise when you finally get to where God is leading you. More often than not, the same degree of struggle you endured on the way up may be the same degree of challenge you experience once you've made it to the peak of your creativity and popularity.

What happens when all the lights are on you? A well-known pastor said something to the effect of a pedestal being a landing where the lights shining on you tend to expose many flaws. But then, when all your flaws are exposed by all the people who put you on this human-elevated plateau, what happens when they turn their backs on you? Are you prepared to handle the success that comes from the manifestation of your dreams?

I would venture to say that the greatest struggle is not in the pit, but when you finally reach the pinnacle. How will you handle life when everybody's coming to you and wanting something, and all eyes are on you?

Well, Joseph finally achieved the success of his dream. He'd dealt with the jealousy and envy of his brothers and ended up thrown into a pit. He'd been sold into slavery. He'd been in Potiphar's house and accused of sexual assault. He'd been thrown in prison. Then he was second-in-command of Egypt. The things he dreamed about when he was seventeen had come to pass . . . many years later.

What happens when God does for you what he did for Joseph or some celebrity or highly successful entrepreneur? What happens when *you* get there?

I'm convinced that what makes or breaks us is not what happens in progress or the pursuit of our dreams. If we're not adequately prepared for that time when our dreams manifest, it's very possible for us to destroy everything we've worked our entire lives to achieve.

Joseph finally made it to the height of his productivity. You would think his struggles were over. But soon he experienced the greatest challenges of his life with the manifestation of his dream. Joseph has just told Pharaoh to spend the seven years of feasting preparing for seven years of famine.

Joseph had finally made it. As Governor of Egypt, he was over everyone, so all those who wanted food had to come through him. And so, unbeknownst to him at the time, his brothers had been sent down to Egypt by their father to get corn.

Egypt was where everybody went to get food when there was none in the land of Canaan. His father Jacob sent ten of his sons to Egypt to buy food, but the youngest, Benjamin, stayed at home. *"And the sons of Israel [Jacob] came to buy corn . . . for the famine was in the land of Canaan. And his brothers came and bowed down themselves before him with their faces to the earth. And Joseph saw his brothers, and he knew them, but made himself strange unto them."*

Joseph had not seen his brothers for more than a decade, so they did not recognize him. This was the start of those challenges Joseph would face once his dream was becoming a reality. By studying Joseph's life, you can deal with your particular challenges after you have achieved the desires God has placed in your heart.

Do Not Repay Wickedness With Wickedness

Joseph's brothers talked roughly to him when he was a teenager with just a coat and a dream. They were so jealous that they couldn't even speak peaceably to him. Now fast forward a few years and the Bible tells us that the tables have been turned: *"And he [Joseph] spake roughly unto them."*

This is a serious challenge you're bound to face when your dream finally becomes a successful reality. You may get the opportunity to return negativity that others directed toward you on your way up. Don't do it. Be very careful not to return wickedness for wickedness. It's possible to be so warped by the people who messed with you on your way up that when your dream manifests, you may be tempted to give them a taste of their own medicine.

Why was Joseph speaking roughly to his brothers? They spoke roughly and not peaceably to him. He looked at them and perhaps thought, *You are the ones who threw me into a pit. I heard you talking about taking my life. But now I've made it. My dream has come to fruition, yet it seems I've still got some unresolved issues within myself.*

When God has elevated or promoted you and your dream has become a reality, don't let the people who jerked you around before you got to that sweet spot cause you to harbor malice in your spirit. Maybe you haven't completely gotten over what they did to you, but the reality is this: Just because someone once threw you into the proverbial pit and said that you weren't going to make it, you shouldn't respond in kind. When you've made it to the top, forget about that pit and focus on your newfound prosperity.

The fact is that whatever the naysayers did or said did not stop you from getting to the place you were ordained to reach. Obviously, all your help was coming from the Lord anyway. God will bless you in spite of the haters.

If you get to the place of your dreams and find that you are still remembering the pain of those who didn't have your back, pray and ask God to show you how to forgive. Let God help you let it go completely. Ask God to fill you, heal you, and make you whole. Don't allow anything to keep you from living the victorious life God promises to those who trust and believe.

I'm thinking that maybe Joseph was struggling with forgiveness. The good thing is that he was even speaking to them at all. Resist the urge to fight fire with fire and wickedness with wickedness. As you may have heard, unforgiveness is like drinking a deadly poison but expecting the other person to die.

And if reaching your dream means that you're delivered from addictions of any kind, stay away from people who are doing what brought you down in the first place. If you've made it to a certain point, you can't be around people who are doing what you used to do. Unfortunately, wickedness has a way of attracting wickedness. You've got to close the door on certain things and never return. Don't do a 'Lot's wife'. Don't look back at the mess God rescued you from.

Make Sure No One Else is Wounded in the Process

"And Joseph remembered his dream." At that point, Joseph decided to play games with his brothers. He said to them, *"You are spies."* (This is probably what I would have said too, if I were him.) He knew good and well that these were his brothers, but he said, *"You have come to see that our land is unprotected."*

But they replied, *"Your servants [we] were twelve brothers, the sons of one man, who lives in the land of Canaan. The youngest is now with our father, and one is no more."*

Ironically, they were talking to the brother they'd gotten rid of, not knowing it was him. This scriptural passage should serve as a warning to you. Be careful how you treat all people, especially your brothers and sisters in Christ. You don't know the influence of those you may be dealing with, or who you'll need one day. The same people you mistreat may have to bring you a glass of water someday. Even though they may look down-and-out now, don't judge them by how they look or what they have. You never know how things are going to turn out for them.

Notice that the brothers didn't say Joseph was dead. Instead, they just said he was 'no more'.

Joseph continued to accuse them of being spies. He was still giving them a hard time, "It's just as I said, you're spies. This is how I'll test you. As Pharaoh lives, you're not going to leave this place until your younger brother comes here. Send one of you to get your brother while the rest of you stay here in jail. We'll see if you're telling the truth or not. As Pharaoh lives, I say you're spies."

Why did Joseph do this? I would think it was because his ten older brothers were birthed by a different mother. The elderly Jacob had two sons by his young, beautiful wife, who died. It stands to reason that every time he looked at his two youngest sons, Joseph and Benjamin, it reminded him that he was still in the game, even though he was a centenarian.

Joseph knew who the other brother was. And he seemed to be motivated by this train of thought: "You guys don't like us because we have different mothers. You first ten are all half-brothers. Sure, you have the same father, but Ben and I have the same mother and father. Maybe since I've been gone, you guys have killed my baby brother, too."

So Joseph told them, *"Do this and you will live, for I fear God."*

When a person realizes a dream, they would be wise not to surround themselves with those who historically are integrity challenged. It would behoove you not to operate out of your emotions when someone approaches you with an offer to help you in business, or to become involved in our personal life. You'd better make sure to fully vet those people you allow into your life.

Let me address single women who may wrongly believe that their biological clock is ticking, to the point of desperation. It is not that much of a stretch to say there are women with this mindset who are ready to rush to the altar at the first sign that a man wants to show them even the slightest bit of attention. It may seem as if your dream to marry is about to come true, and maybe it is. But you'd do well to look into his past before walking into what you think is the manifestation of your dream.

Really, ladies, if he has children by more than one woman and isn't doing his part financially, why would you consider jumping into that situation? If he's not taking care of his responsibilities, what makes you think that when he gets with you, it will be any different? Don't be too eager to get into a relationship with a man before you have at least some idea of who he may have hurt or abandoned on his way to you.

Even with your dreams of entering into business success, it's a good idea to start asking for relationship résumés. You just may be attempting to do business with someone who has a history of changing jobs all the time. This person may already have convinced you that they can help you bring your future into existence. Use godly wisdom and check into their background to make sure they don't have a history of sabotaging those they are close to. Those in pain tend to inflict pain on others. Make sure this is not a case of someone who has wounded others in business or been wounded themselves.

Through his actions, Joseph is really saying, "Let me make sure my little brother has been taken care of before I let you into my life. Tell you what I'm going to do. I'm going to keep you guys here in jail."

"And he put them all together in jail for three days." (Genesis 42:17)

Now, was Joseph wrong to incarcerate his brothers for three days? Some may suggest that he was entertaining thoughts of revenge. I don't think so. After all, he didn't have to offer to help them out. He continues to not want them to know he's well aware of who they are.

By incarcerating them, he's actually saying, "If you bring your little brother back to me, your word will be verified and you shall not die." He's showing himself to be like most of us, a human being struggling with his humanity. He's doing the best he can under the circumstances.

"Then they started talking among themselves. 'Now we're paying for what we did to our brother — we saw how terrified he was when he was begging us for mercy. We wouldn't listen to him and now we're the ones in trouble.' Reuben broke in. 'Didn't I tell you, "Don't hurt the boy"? But no, you wouldn't listen. And now we're paying for his murder.'" (Genesis 42:21-22 MSG)

Don't Speak the Same Language as Your Enemy

Joseph used an interpreter when he spoke with his brothers, so they had no idea that he understood everything they said. Joseph was speaking an Egyptian dialect, but his brothers were still speaking in Hebrew, their native tongue. Joseph understood Hebrew as well, but he acted as if he didn't know what they were saying.

The lesson learned here? There are times when you have to speak on a different level than the people who have tried to kill you or your dreams in the past. You've got to have another language, because when you're dealing with the enemy, it will help you gain the victory. Sometimes you have to speak on a higher level, so it's a blessing to have another language. When the enemy comes and tells you, "You're going to die," you've got to know another language in which to say, "It isn't over until God says it's over." When the enemy tells you, "You're not going to make it," you need another language in which to say, *"Weeping shall endure for the night, but joy comes in the morning."* (Psalm 30:5)

You've got to have wisdom, which to me means that you can't talk the same way your enemy does. You have to speak the language of God's Word. If you find yourself between a rock and a hard place like Joseph was, things can get so rough that you don't know what to say. Just do what Romans 8:26 says: *"For sometimes we know not what to pray for as we should. But the Spirit helps us in our infirmities, for when we know not what to pray for, the Spirit makes intercession with groanings that cannot be uttered."*

When you're on the job and people are trying to tear you up, for instance, just groan, and the Holy Spirit will step in and say, *"Fret not yourself because of evildoers."* (Psalm 37:1)

Realize There are Some Battles You Can't Fight in the Flesh

One of the jobs of the Holy Spirit is to make intercession for the saints. In the New Testament, He is called the 'Paraclete', which literally means 'one who comes alongside'. Now maybe you've never heard that term because you don't know Greek, but you *have* heard the word 'paramedic'. If you're driving on the interstate and another car hits you and causes you bodily harm, you can dial 911 and call for a paramedic, who will come to your aid to assist you on the way to the hospital. Sometimes the Holy Spirit is not just the Paraclete, but also a paramedic. When you've been hurt in life, you can call on the Paraclete, who will act like a paramedic and treat life's wounds.

You know that to 'paraphrase' is to say something in a different way. Thank God for our Paraclete, who's not just a paramedic, but also a paraphraser. You might be praying, "God, give me a saved husband," but the Holy Spirit says, "No, you don't need a saved husband. You need to save your credit rating first." He knows you're not ready to be an asset because you're still a liability.

You may not have heard of a Paraclete, paramedic, or paraphrase, but you *have* heard of a parachute. If you're flying in an airplane that's about to crash, you may have the benefit of a parachute so that when you jump out of the plane, the balloon mechanism will keep you from falling. Just like a parachute, the Holy Spirit catches you when you start to tumble.

When you achieve your dream, there will be times when you need someone else to speak for you. Even when you get to your peak level, problems and troublesome situations of life will come, so you're going to need somebody to intercede for you when you can't speak for yourself. You need an intercessor who will stand in the gap. I believe that interpreter for Joseph is an Old Testament foreshadowing of a New Testament dispensation — the Holy Spirit.

Release Your Emotions

"Joseph turned away from them and cried." He was probably weeping because of the pain of his past. You may be a world-famous celebrity, but just because you've made it and your dream has come to pass doesn't mean bad memories from your past won't still affect you, causing moments of sorrow. So Joseph retreated into his inner chamber as he became full of emotion while dealing with what had happened to him. He stole away to a secret place to let it all out.

You will not be fully healed emotionally until you acknowledge what has happened to you. Just because you've made it doesn't mean that what others did to you wasn't real.

You can be favored, but you still haven't forgotten how you were mistreated. You may have to get away and say, "You know what? I need to let this out. Let me stop trying to fake it and deal with the fact that I've been hurt. I've got some issues, but it's not about what people think of me right now; it's about getting in touch."

You may have to confess, "God, I have some major issues — stuff I haven't been healed from. I've tried to put it out of my mind, but maybe I haven't really forgiven the ones who have hurt me. I've got to let stuff go today. I can't go into the future until I get rid of all this baggage."

One of my friends was experiencing the vision problems that inevitably come with age. He realized that he could no longer see as well as he once did. So he went to the optometrist, who examined his eyes. My friend thought he would need glasses or retinal surgery, but the doctor simply gave him a prescription for eyedrops to enable him to produce tears. His eyesight issues were caused by dryness, and that prescribed medication helped him to see better.

You may have been hurt years ago and wonder why you're still crying. You may say to yourself, "I should be over that, but it still upsets me. Why am I still thinking about how someone abused me? Why am I still crying over how my daddy walked out of my life if I'm grown now? Why am I still upset over the mistakes someone else made?"

Think of those shed tears as a way to get rid of whatever may be obstructing your spiritual and emotional vision. After you've cried those tears, God will enable you to see things more clearly. Your life will improve after you release a little water to wash away your pain. A good cry works wonders, as long as it doesn't bring on a pity party.

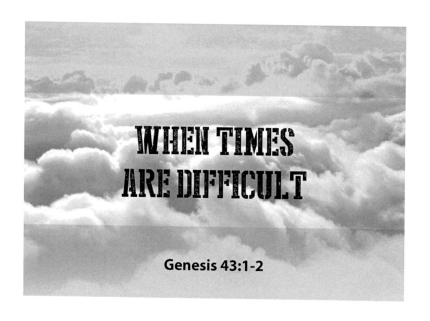

WHEN TIMES ARE DIFFICULT

Genesis 43:1-2

A rid conditions had ravaged the lands of Egypt and Canaan. Production, trade, and the gross national product were at all-time lows. Food was scarce in the land. This ancient recession had rendered the people helpless and hopeless. Only the ingenious and prophetic leadership of Joseph made a food supply available. It was a difficult situation that can be described as an act of God. A providential directive of retributive justice had ensured that the clouds would not give forth water to bring liquid refreshment to their crops and cattle, which began to perish. Agriculture and farming suffered. Families did what they could to survive.

Joseph's brothers had no idea that their own survival would be linked to the dreamer they had once discarded.

Genesis 43 is relevant to where we are now, as a country. The recession and unemployment figures, coupled with major corporations filing for bankruptcy or closing their doors altogether, is strikingly similar to what Jacob and his family were going through. Many of us know how it feels to deal with life-and-death struggles. We live in a day and time in which people seem to find difficulty just surviving. There's an ongoing search for effective leadership to provide the answers for the maladies in our society. Depression has overwhelmed people to the point of apathy, not only in secular societies but among sacred communities, as well.

What happens when you are dissatisfied with your job but because of the state of the economy and the job market, you find yourself settling and simply surviving? What do you do when you find yourself in a situation in which you want to live, but it seems that you don't have the strength or supply to survive?

Jacob's entire family was struggling, yet since they were connected to the dreamer, their actions in the midst of turmoil can encourage you to look beyond the despair. It's imperative to learn survival lessons when times are difficult.

Be Transparent About Your Reality

"And the famine was sore in the land. And it came to pass, when they had eaten up the corn, which they had brought up out of the land of Egypt, that their father said to them, Go again."

Jacob was going through his own desperate moment of struggle, crisis, and recession. This was not happening to him because he was disconnected from God or because God was punishing the entire nation. No, this arduous trial occurred due to the natural ebb and flow of life itself. Even though Jacob was connected to Abraham — through whose seed God had promised to bless all the nations of the Earth — he wasn't exempt from going through a situation of extreme difficulty.

This vital passage teaches that even though you're connected to Christ, are the darling of His eye, and He has given you a promise, you will still eventually find yourself at a place in your life when what you thought you needed to survive may not be there. It does not mean you don't love God, or that He's paying you back for a sin you committed.

But what happens when, in spite of the fact that you love God, you are going through a difficult time and find yourself in need? The text says the famine 'was sore in the land' and 'they had eaten up all the corn'. Essentially, they didn't have any food supply or means to produce it in Canaan.

But notice that Jacob didn't say, "When we're broke and don't have corn, don't worry about it. Let's just fake it 'til we make it." He didn't say that when they stopped having groceries in the pantry, they would just spin around three times and call on the name of Jesus. He didn't say when they had anything less or insignificant, "I'm too anointed to be disappointed. I'm too blessed to be stressed. Hallelujah, anyhow." He came to the point when he said, "You know what? We are connected to God, but here's what's real. We don't have enough to eat."

Part of the problem with the Word of Faith movement and some of the preaching you may have heard is that people have been taught that if they speak words into the atmosphere, their situation will automatically change. Yet nothing could be further from the truth.

We've got to stop telling people that they're going to be rich and everyone will enjoy prosperity. Jesus said, *"The poor you'll have with you always."* Preachers can't go to parts of Africa and tell the people there that money is coming. Those people are just trying to survive one day at a time.

When you go to the doctor and he says you have a spot on your lung or prostrate, that isn't the time to say, "I'm just going to fake it 'til I make it," or, "I'm not claiming that." That's the moment when you say to yourself, "I see what the results say. I know what the doctors say, and I'm not going to bury my head in the sand. I'm going to change my diet if necessary. If chemotherapy and radiation are required, I know that God is so awesome, He can work through medical science. I'm going to do my part and be real about where I am, because if I just fake it 'til I make it, I may not make it, because it means I'm not being real. I'm going to follow the doctor's orders and do what the nurses have said, but even as I follow medical science, I understand this: The end of my life is not based on what medical science says, because even the best doctor is only practicing medicine. I recognize, however, that I can't fix what I cannot face."

Look at yourself in the mirror and say, "You know what? My finances are in disarray. I'm spending money that I don't have, trying to impress people I don't even like, who are going to talk about me regardless of what I'm wearing. Here is where I am in my life. It looks bleak and bad, but I'm going to accept that reality and be transparent about where I am because I understand this: I cannot fix my problem until I'm willing to deal with it."

One of the first issues is that we've got be real with ourselves and have people around us who are real. Sometimes we can love our friends so much that we just want them to be happy, so we act like things are better than they really are. In other words, if I'm your friend and you know I'm struggling with drug or alcohol abuse, I don't need you to offer me a glass of champagne. Instead, I need you, as my friend, to go to the store and pick up some milk, apple cider, or green tea for me. I need you to be real about my situation and say, "Because I love you as my friend and this is your weakness, I'll tell you what I'm going to do. I won't even drink around you because I know you can't handle it." That's what real friends do.

God has put people in our lives who can be real with us. They're the ones who can honestly tell us things we need to hear, such as, "Why are you running into that relationship? It doesn't offer you anything. It's dead. It doesn't push you to the next level. It's parasitic and not helpful."

Lack of transparency and reality is a major problem in the church. There seems to be so much hypocrisy and judgment in our congregations today. In fact, throughout my life, I've discovered that the worst people are pharisaical church members who can only point out others' struggles, flaws, and frailties.

A famous actor gave a very impassioned, heartfelt eulogy about the struggles of a fellow celebrity who had just passed. During the televised eulogy, he let a profanity slip out. I'm so sure that the judgmental 'saints' watching probably said to themselves, "Oh, Lord! God's going to strike him down. He shouldn't embarrass himself like that in the house of the Lord."

Why is it so many of us can judge a person for letting a word slip in church and then get garbage-mouthed as soon as we get to the parking lot after service? Let's be real about this. Out of all the beautiful things he said, the main thing that was reported in the media was the misstatement he made in the pulpit. I would venture to say that a few of the church folks who criticized him were sitting on a pocket full of lottery tickets.

I ask you, what difference does it make? Why do those of us who call ourselves children of the King categorize sin as if there is some kind of hierarchy, as if some sinful behaviors are worse than others? The reality is that all of us are struggling with something, and if not for the grace of God, we would all be condemned. All of us need the same grace.

You must be transparent about your reality. Like Jacob, you have to say, "Here's where I am in my life. There's famine in the land, and we don't have what we need to survive." You have to stop trying to be what you're not. You're transparent when you can look at yourself and say, "Here's who I am. I'm not trying to make myself look like I'm the greatest, most wonderful person when I've got struggles just like anyone else."

Be Thankful That You Still Have Resources

Jacob's sons returned from Egypt with supplies, but soon they were all gone. Jacob said, "Go back to Egypt and buy us some food."

Maybe it went something like this: "You know what? Because of our reality, I cannot expect to have much right now. But I'm still content, even though we don't have any corn left. I know that if we don't do something now, we'll die. The true blessing is that everything we have is not gone. The enemy or storm may have taken a lot from us, but we still have a little bit to buy food."

You should praise God that, despite all that has been taken from you, you've still got enough to survive. You may not be able to eat filet mignon, but you can eat ground beef. You should thank God that even though the enemy may have taken your home and family, you still have a little something left. Thank Him that you still have your peace of mind and joy, which is something the Enemy can't take from you. You may have lost your checkbook or even your 401(k), but the Devil can't take your peace of mind, joy, or praise unless you hand it over.

If you should lose everything but still have Jesus, you have enough to start over again. The Lord woke you up this morning, gave you health and strength. You were clothed, and in your right mind. Praise God not for what you lost, but for what you have left. You've got to understand the trick of the

Devil: He'll make you focus on what you've lost and who walked out of your life. But you've got to make up your mind that you're not going to do that anymore. You need to stop going through old pictures. You're having a pity party, not wanting to come to the singles' class because you're still in mourning. Instead, you'd better say, "I've still got something left. Maybe God took that person out of my life because He has something better for me. Any way, You bless me. . ."

One of the greatest lessons I've ever learned in my life was one my mother taught me when I was a young boy. She said, "When you get on your knees, say this prayer: 'Our Father, which art in heaven, hallowed be Thy name. Thy Kingdom come; Thy will be done, on Earth as it is in Heaven.'" I didn't understand this as a boy, but I can now say the next line when I'm going through the worst kind of crisis, vacillating in my own emotions, and unable to sleep: 'Give us this day our daily bread.'

Stop worrying about next month. Stop worrying about how you're going to pay your child's tuition in college in three years. Just say, "God, give me what I need." You can sleep at night if you take it one day at a time. If He took care of you yesterday, He can take care of you tomorrow. Why are you worried? Take your mind off what you can't handle and thank God for those things you can do for yourself.

You may ask, "What happens if I get cancer? What am I going to do about that? What's going to happen when my hair starts falling out?" Why are you worrying about what's unknown? Be thankful that you still have something. It may not be what you want or where you want to be, but it could be worse than it is right now.

Be Truthful and Righteous, Even in a Recession.

Jacob said, "Go buy us a little food."

In my mind, Judah replied, "But Dad, remember last time we were there? He asked us about our father and brother. We told him we had a little brother, so he kept one of our brothers for ransom and told us that he wasn't going to let him go until we brought back our baby brother. And so, Dad, we know that you love your baby boy Benjamin, but there's no need for us to go ask for food if we don't bring him with us."

Jacob responded, "Are you trying to kill me? Are you trying to bring me down and destroy my heart? Why did you even tell him you had another brother?"

Judah said, "We didn't know he would ask all those questions. If you send Benjamin with us, we'll go and do it. But there's no need to go unless we bring our little brother."

Jacob told them to take the best fruits, vegetables, honey, balm, and other spices, and twice the money they found in their sacks. He wanted them to double what Joseph had given them. "Take the money back to him in case it was a mistake. Don't lose your integrity."

In the Bible, Jacob continued: *"And take also your brother [Benjamin], and arise, go again unto the man. And I'm praying to God Almighty that He'll give you mercy from this man."*

He didn't know this man was his own son, Joseph. He was saying, "Go to this man and ask for mercy so that he might send your other brother and Benjamin back. And if I'm bereaved of my children, so let it be."

"And the men took that present, and they took double money in their hand. . . and stood before Joseph."

Be Totally Convinced That You Will be Rescued

Judah said, *"Send Benjamin with me, and we will arise and go; that we may live, and not die."* In other words, he's saying, "I know that you're worried he's going to kill Benjamin, Reuben, or Simeon. But if you let Benjamin come down to Egypt with me ('praise'), I'm convinced that we will live and not die."

No matter what you're going through, you've got to be like Judah. You've got to say to yourself, "No matter what it looks like, I'm convinced that if I take praise with me and if I stay rooted in the will of the King, I shall live and not die." You need to prophesy over yourself that you shall live and not die. When people are trying to build a case against you so you'll be fired from your job, say you shall live and not die. If you're going to the doctor's office this week, make sure you take praise with you.

Romans 8:38-39 says, *"For I am persuaded, that neither death, nor life, nor angels, nor principalities, nor powers, nor things present, nor things to come, nor height, nor depth, nor any other creature, shall be able to separate us from the love of God, which is in Christ Jesus our Lord."*

Judah was telling Jacob, "Dad, we shall live and not die. I don't know how or when God is going to fix it, but I believe in my own spirit that no matter what we're going through, we shall live and not die."

"And when Joseph saw Benjamin with them, he said to the ruler of the house, Bring these men home and slay a calf and make ready because we're going to eat together at noon."

In this passage, Joseph was a symbolic picture of God. When Joseph saw Benjamin, can't you just hear him telling his servants, "I don't want these boys to die or let them think they're going to die. I know they were jealous of me and threw me into the pit. I know that I had fourteen years of hard times because of these bad brothers of mine, but because of the grace of God, don't kill them. I'm going to bring them into the king's house, but before they come in, somebody has to kill the fatted calf."

Just because you have accepted Jesus Christ as your Lord and personal Savior, and you're saved, doesn't mean you won't have any struggles. It may not be drugs or alcohol, but you might struggle with your own spirituality, family, sexuality, job, health, or marriage. Don't be convinced that the struggle will take you out. Just keep singing, "Jesus loves me, this I know, for the Bible tells me so. . ."

Just like Joseph's brothers, we have all made mistakes. There are things we did wrong before we got saved. Since we've been saved, we still have needs in our lives. But we should be glad that when the Lord could have killed us for our wrongdoing, He didn't.

On the holiday we commemorate as Good Friday, the Lamb of God was dragged up Calvary Hill, where they hanged Him high and stretched Him wide. He hung down His head and died for all sinners. Because the Lamb died, we have a right to the Tree of Life. Because the Lamb died, we can run through troops and leap over walls. Because the Lamb died, He'll help us truly live and make our enemies leave us alone. Because the Lamb died, we're going to make it. Because the Lamb died, one of these days we're going to dine at the Master's table. When it's all over, we're bound for Mt. Zion to view the Holy City.

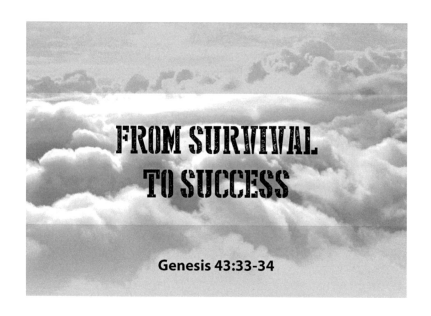

FROM SURVIVAL TO SUCCESS

Genesis 43:33-34

The seven years of famine was indeed a difficult time for Hebrews and Egyptians alike. Although the Egyptians had serious issues with the Hebrews, the reality was that all of them were in the same boat because of the difficult economic conditions in which they lived.

And so God elevated Joseph, a Hebrew by culture, to second-in-command over all of Egypt, subject only to Pharaoh. After He lifted him from prison, God's purpose for Joseph had come to fruition. God allowed Joseph to interpret the Pharaoh's dream and help him understand that seven years of surplus would be followed by seven years of famine. His ingenious and prophetic ministry allowed the Egyptian nation to make sure they had their pantries stocked so that when the time of famine arose, the people in the land would have food.

Now the conditions caused people to leave Canaan to go to Egypt because only the Egyptians had a sufficient supply of food. Jacob (also known as Israel) had already sent his sons on one journey there to get food. They returned home to Canaan, leaving Simeon in the Egyptian jail as collateral until they could bring Benjamin back with them. The family's food had dissipated. Rather than see his family die from starvation, Jacob acquiesced to their request to take their baby brother, Benjamin, back to Egypt with them, because he realized that if they went back this time without his youngest son, that promised supply of food would not be forthcoming.

They made a 250-mile journey from Canaan to Egypt to get food. When the brothers got there, Joseph did not kill them. Instead, he allowed a fatted animal to be killed and invited them to join him at his table for lunch. These brothers had no idea what was about to unfold in their lives. They were just trying to survive. Yet through the grace and favor of God, and Joseph's benevolence, they were able to gain a sense that survival is possible.

Child of God, understand that God doesn't mean for you to merely survive. God wants you to thrive, prosper, and enjoy success. 3 John 2 says, *"Beloved, I wish above all things that you prosper and be in health, even as your soul prospers."*

When using the term 'prosperity', I don't mean that everyone is going to be a millionaire, or that no one will face any challenges or issues in life. There are times in your life when God will literally lead you to a place where nothing is broken or missing. You can and will arrive at that place in your life when you have true peace, contentment, and a sense of tranquility, regardless of what you're facing.

At the beginning of Genesis 43, Jacob's family moved from a place of survival to a place of success. This is what's currently happening during this season in our country. For the last three or four years, many of us have just been surviving. The job market has been down, and adjustable rate mortgages and foreclosure rates have gone through the roof. Gas prices are back up to almost $4 a gallon.

In the midst of these difficult economic times, it's hard to find sufficient supply. You may be struggling just to make it from week to week and paycheck to paycheck. At times it may seem like hope is unavailable. You may be of the mindset that the federal government appears to be more concerned with Wall Street than Main Street. Because of 'banksters' who some feel have destroyed the economy to satisfy their own greed, you may be one of those who feels trapped in a desperate place of mere survival.

While I thank God for survival, I sense that the virgin moments of success are on the horizon, and things are getting ready to happen that will turn it all around for you and for the country. With everything in my spirit, over the next year or so I believe that, regarding those things we've been dealing with, God has already manifested in the spiritual what He's going to allow to come into fruition in the natural. God wants to shift you from a moment of just surviving to a moment of success. This will be the moment when you don't have to pace up and down the floor, worrying about paying the mortgage this month. God is shifting the country from a place of survival to a place where nothing is missing or broken.

Have faith that where you are right now is not how you're going to spend the rest of your days. You're holding on to the expectation that God is going to make this major shift in your circumstances, but you've got to be ready for that time when the shift comes so that you won't deal with the opportunity improperly. When God gives you that moment and turns on the bright lights, you've got to act as if you have some sense to handle it. When you get on the big stage, you need to be ready for your spiritual close-up. You should be able to say, "God, You've given me great opportunities because I was faithful over a little, and You can make me a ruler over much."

But what do you do when God has already shifted you from survival to success? How can you make sure you will be ready for prime time when your breakthrough shows up? How can you maximize that moment so you make the same about-face as Jacob's family?

Here are a few ways you can learn from their situation.

Stop Agonizing in the Face of Breakthrough

Joseph told his servant to prepare an animal and let his brothers know that they were going to dine with him at his house at noon. *"And the servant did as Joseph bade, and the servant brought the men into Joseph's house."*

Here's where it gets interesting. They had been trying to survive by going down to Egypt to buy food, yet they didn't know Joseph was their brother. He said something similar to the following, "Since y'all have brought Benjamin, the baby brother, I'm not going to just allow you to survive. I'm not just going to give you bags of corn and send you back on that 250-mile journey to Canaan. I'm going to bring you into my royal chambers, spread out a banquet for you, and allow you to dine with me at my table."

God was apparently shifting Joseph's brothers from mere survival to abundant success. Those men were on the brink of success and in the presence of royalty. But verse 18 says, *"And the men were afraid, because they were brought into Joseph's house."*

When God answers your prayer by opening a door, don't mishandle the blessing because you're afraid of success. Instead, allow yourself to bask in the glorious reality of what is about to manifest.

I'm talking to you, my sister in Christ. You've been praying for a husband. You're tired of being alone, and it looks like God has answered your prayer. He has sent a hard-working, Christ-loving man into your life to have a relationship with you. He wants to spend time with you, so he asks you for your phone number, but you decide you can't meet him for lunch or go to the movies with him. You're acting as if you're not interested, as if your dance card is too full to accommodate another suitor. You want to maintain an aura of coolness, although you're really very much interested in the prospect of someone in your life.

But rather than pray, "God, give me discernment," you give him a hard time because someone from your past did you wrong. You won't let yourself open up to the possibility of a new relationship. Could it be that because you've been hurt before, you're afraid to trust someone and love again? Can't you see that God may have sent the answer to your prayer?

You should choose to say, "God, when You're shifting me from survival to success by sending me my blessing, don't let me be so intimidated by the blessing that I shut down. God, show me that this is of You. Give me the wisdom to jump in with my heart and my head, and with prudence. Let me know that it's You so that I can properly handle the blessing."

Perhaps God is trying to get you to start a business — to step out, relocate, and walk in your dream. Don't get so comfortable in survival mode that you're afraid to take that leap of faith and see what it feels like to enjoy success.

There are men who work so hard because they've heard horror stories of the Great Depression. You hoard money or maybe delay enjoying the fruits of your labor because you don't want to open your wallet for fear that your savings will fly away. Those who know you accuse you of being miserly and unable to joyfully live life to the fullest if spending money is involved. Don't misunderstand. There's nothing wrong with being prudent in your finances or saving your money for a rainy day. However, be free to enjoy yourself once in a while and experience the life God has given us richly to enjoy.

Joseph's brothers had just received a picture of redemption and a promise of repast and fellowship because an animal had been killed. But in spite of all this, the text says that they were afraid. They were trying to figure it all out, asking each other, "Oh, why did we get invited to a dinner? What's going to happen now? Maybe something's going on."

The same thing happened in another part of the Bible when the woman with an issue of blood heard that Jesus was coming through the streets. She said to herself, "If I can just touch the hem of His garment, I'll be made well." She managed to touch His clothes, *"And straightway the fountain of her blood was dried up; and she felt in her body that she was healed of that plague."*

Jesus said, *"Who touched me?"*

"But the woman fearing and trembling, knowing what was done in her, came and fell down before him, and told him all the truth."

Jesus told her, *"Go in peace."* In other words, "Woman, why are you afraid and trembling when you just got healed?"

The time for fear and trembling shouldn't have been after her healing, but before. If you've been touched and delivered by the hand of God, how can you be afraid when you've been healed and received your breakthrough? You should say to the Enemy and everyone else, "I will not walk in fear once God has given me the deliverance and provided my breakthrough for me." That's not the time to walk in fear, but to walk in boldness. Hold your head up high and say, *"He whom the Son sets free is free indeed."* (John 8:36)

It also happened when Peter and John went to the tomb on Sunday morning after Jesus had been resurrected from the grave. John 20:3 says that Peter ran into the tomb first. He looked inside where he 'saw the linen clothes lying'. Jesus was not in the tomb because He had already risen. Peter and John ran back to tell the other disciples, and they believed that Jesus had been resurrected from the dead.

The two were at the place of breakthrough, yet verse 11 says, *"But Mary stood without at the sepulchre weeping: and as she wept, she stooped down, and looked into the sepulchre."* Mary was also at the place of breakthrough, but she was agonizing and weeping. Peter, on the other hand, looked in, and both he and John believed.

When you are on the brink of success, propose in your heart not to focus on everything that could go possibly wrong. Instead, you should say, "God, any way You bless me, I'll be satisfied. I'm not going to be at the place of breakthrough, agonizing right here, but then the breakthrough happens over there and I'll miss it." When God brings you to a place of deliverance, make a point not to agonize in the face of breakthrough.

Stop Apologizing for Your Blessings

But they became anxious when they were brought into Joseph's home, thinking, "It's the money. He thinks we ran off with the money on our first trip down here. And now he's got us where he wants us — he's going to turn us into slaves and confiscate our donkeys."

When the brothers went to Egypt the first time to buy corn, Joseph ordered his servants to put the money they had spent on the food back into their bags. The brothers didn't discover it until they got home. For the second time, Jacob told his sons to take the money back because he didn't want his sons to be thought of as thieves. So as they were coming into Joseph's house, they were probably wondering, "You know what? We must be coming here because he thinks we ran off with that money our first time down here. And what is he going to do to us?"

Recently, I watched a television commercial for an insurance company that showed a man downstairs at home in the wee hours of the morning, pajama-clad and talking on the phone. His wife, convinced that he was having a late night tête-à-tête with a female, came downstairs and snatched the phone from him. She said, "What's your name? What are you wearing?" The voice on the other end replied, "I'm Jake, and I'm wearing khakis and a red shirt." The wife told her husband, "She sounds hideous!" The husband responded, "Well, that's because she's a guy." He was talking to his male insurance agent the entire time about savings.

That's just to illustrate how you may allow the Devil to play tricks on your imagination and make you paranoid about problems that don't exist. You might even do this when God has brought you to a place of breakthrough. Why is it that some of us expect the negative? Men question their spouses when out in public and mistakenly accuse their wives of flirting with other men as they walk past them. Good thing your 'virtuous woman' knows how to handle foolishness such as that and politely but firmly puts you in your place.

Joseph's worried brothers said, "Oh, no. Maybe he's going to put us in jail." They went to Joseph's steward and told him, in so many words, "Listen, we came down here a little while ago to buy some food. On our way home the very first night we left, we opened our bags and what we discovered was the same money we spent to buy the food. We don't know how that money got back in our bags, but we didn't steal it. We paid for that food fair and square, and we brought the same amount of money back, along with more money with us for food. We don't know who put that money in our bags. We didn't do it, sir."

In today's lingo, it's as if they're saying, "We didn't do anything crazy. We weren't in collusion with the cashier. It's not as if we wrote a check, got the merchandise, and then canceled the check. We didn't write the check to the store from an account that's been closed for two months. We didn't buy suits, leave the tags on them, wear them for a while, and then take them back." Sound familiar?

But the steward said, "Everything is in order, don't worry. Your God and the God of your father must have given you a bonus."

There have been instances when God blessed you with material things, but you weren't able to fully enjoy what you got because you were too busy trying to justify to friends and family how and why you were the recipient of God's bounty. Rather than tell your envious neighbors and relatives that what you purchased was 'on sale' to appease them, let them know how thankful you are about what the Lord has done for you. Similarly, you may even have been hesitant about driving your new car because you don't want others to label you as a showoff. Listen, when God blesses you, stop living your life trying to make people accept you.

I'll never forget when, during my first pastorate, I bought a new car but was reluctant to drive it to church. I'd never taken any money from anywhere that I did not earn. I paid the note myself and purchased the car with my personal funds, but I didn't want the congregation to get the wrong impression. I had been driving my mother's car, leaving mine home in the garage, when I heard the Lord in my spirit. He asked me what the problem was, and this is how I responded, "Lord, if I drive my new Acura to church, they'll stop paying their tithes and offerings. They'll say this or that." The Lord said, "Let Me tell you something. When I'm blessing you, don't let anyone make you hide what I'm doing in your life. The same people who are going to talk about you for driving a luxury car talked negatively about you when your compact car kept breaking down."

When God blesses you, don't apologize for your blessing. Stop trying to justify how you got what you got. Just say, "I'm blessed, and I'm one of the blessed. If you can't stand my blessing, that's your problem, not mine." Folks may say, "He's changing. He's acting differently." Maybe they're projecting the way they would respond on to you. Just look all the naysayers in the eye with your head held high and say, "I'm the same person I've always been. I'm just grateful for what God has done in my life."

Joseph's brothers tried to justify their blessing by denying it ever happened. "We don't know how that stuff got in our bag," they said. In my mind, the servant gave the best answer, "When you got stuff in your bag that you didn't deserve and don't know how it got there, don't try to apologize for it. Just say, 'The Lord must have given me a bonus.' "

Are you expecting a bonus? Are you anticipating that God will send unexpected income, a better job, or maybe a raise? Be prepared to tell people, "If you can't handle me now, you surely won't be able to handle me when my bonus comes, because I'm going to raise my hands in the air while shouting and praising God."

God can even give you a double bonus because He's able to bless us "exceeding abundantly above all that we can ask or think." So when someone asks you how you got your job and suggests that you must have known someone in the company, tell them it's a bonus from God. When someone compliments you on your appearance, tell them it's a bonus from God. And when they question how you're able to buy a house in this bad economy, joyfully reply that your house is a bonus, and you serve a bonus-giving God!

Stop Analyzing. Just Receive God's Best

Joseph's servant let the brothers know that they need not be fearful. He told them that he was told by Joseph to bring them into the palace. *"Peace be to you; fear not. . . . Let me also bring out your brother Simeon — the one we kept as collateral since your first visit."*

"And the man brought the men into Joseph's house. He gave them water and they washed their feet." The water Joseph had his servant provide may have had a deeper spiritual significance than just wanting them to be clean. Joseph was essentially saying, "I want you to wash your feet, boys, not just because of the dust you've picked up on the way from Canaan to Egypt, but as a symbolic gesture to wash away the dirt you did to me those many years ago."

Then the servant gave their donkeys some feed and the brothers got their gifts ready. *"When Joseph came home, they brought him the presents and bowed down."* Compare this to his dreams.

"And then he asked them of their welfare and said, 'Is your father well?'" Jacob's sons didn't know this was their brother whom they had sold into slavery. They hadn't seen him in fourteen years, so they had no idea this was Joseph.

Joseph *"lifted up his eyes and saw his brother Benjamin."* He got so choked up that he had to run into another room just to shed some tears because his brother was alive. He was so excited that they had not killed his baby brother. The text goes further to say that he *". . . washed his face and went out, and refrained himself. . ."* Joseph, strong man that he was, apparently had no problem shedding tears of joy. He went away from his brothers to let it all out and then came back and told the servants to set the table.

Every man should be strong enough to shed tears when overcome. Every man should be able to admit to himself that there are times when he needs to just get away, give in to his emotions, and let go of pain, grief, or overwhelming joy.

"And they set one for him by himself, and for them by themselves." They put the Egyptians at one table and the Hebrews at another. Back then, Egyptians didn't eat with Hebrews because they believed that sitting at the table with them was somewhat of an abomination. Joseph was forced to seat his brothers at a table apart from him, but he was able to look directly on them.

The eleven brothers were seated chronologically, from the oldest to the youngest. They looked at each other, and the text says, *"They marveled."* Why? Because he seated them according to their ages. The odds of Joseph seating them correctly without knowing them must have been 40,000,000:1.

Joseph arranged his brothers in order because of the socially-accepted inheritance laws during that time. The blessing was supposed to go from the firstborn to the last. Since, as Christians, we're all the King's kids, there's no need for us to spend time and energy trying to figure out who is first in His eyes.

Stop Envying What's on Someone Else's Plate

"When the brothers' plates were served from Joseph's table, Benjamin's plate came piled high, far more so than his brothers. And so the brothers feasted with Joseph, drinking freely."

These brothers, unbeknownst to them, were getting ready to have dinner as a family for the first time in years. Joseph gave them all something to eat and blessed them from his table. So he didn't have his own food at the head table and a different chef for their table; everything that was on Joseph's plate was on theirs as well. They were eating the same thing.

Similarly, do you not know that everything in the Kingdom is yours? In Matthew 16:19, Jesus said, *"I give unto you the keys of the kingdom; and whatsoever you bind on earth will be bound in heaven."*

When my wife and I were first married, we dined with her family. It surprised me that when the server came to take our order, everyone at the table inquired of the others what they planned to eat. I wasn't used to that. In my family, you just ordered what you wanted without discussing it with everyone seated. It took awhile for the food choice conferences to end, and the server ended up having to come back to our table several times before we were ready.

After what seemed like an eternity of going around the table, I realized that no two people ordered the same thing. I was seated next to my mother-in-law and noticed her hand coming toward my plate. To say that I was surprised is an understatement. I then noticed that everyone at the table had their forks in someone else's plate. My family didn't do that, and I was starting to become frustrated. I mean, who does that?

That's when the voice of God came up in my spirit, "Whatever is on your plate, when it's family and the food is really blessing them, you don't have to be eating the same thing." That's why you should thank God when you have real friends in your life. You know you'll never starve, because they always have something on their plate to share with you.

All of Joseph's brothers were eating, but the baby boy Benjamin's plate was piled five times higher than the others. Joseph was showing honor to his baby brother and testing his other brothers. He was basically saying, "You guys threw me into a pit because I had a dream that was different from yours. So your jealousy couldn't handle my dream. Now let me see how you're going to respond when somebody else at the same table gets a little bit more on their plate than you do."

One of the best life lessons for you to learn is to not envy what other people have on their plates. I'm thinking some Christians, had they been in Joseph's brothers' shoes at the feast, would have immediately stopped eating and said, "Hey, I'm older than he is. He wasn't even supposed to come in the first place! Why did you give him more than me?"

It's sad that some people cannot handle when it appears as if someone else has more than they do. That's especially true among family and friends. In fact, it's even true about some preachers. We get around each other and love to embellish on what we've preached to our congregations.

A pastor once told me, "Yeah, Doc, I really killed 'em yesterday at church."

I replied, "That's the problem. You've been killing 'em and not giving 'em life."

It's a constant contest to see who has the most members, largest church building, nicest car, best suits, and yada, yada, yada. The problem is that we can't handle our plate, so we've got to show it off to make people think we're more than we actually are.

Have you ever seen one of those reality shows in which celebrities go to poverty-stricken Third World countries and have the audacity to take dozens of pairs of shoes with them? People there don't even have *one* pair, for goodness' sake. When your heart is in the right place and your motive is to help and serve, you need only take a single pair on your journey. You should be confident enough to know that it's not the shoes that make you (even if cameras are recording your every move); it's you and your attitude of compassion that make the shoes.

It doesn't matter what you wear or drive. When God puts something in you, it's going to show up on the outside. So instead of worrying about who has and has not, or who's doing this and who's doing that, tell yourself, "I've learned how to simply enjoy what's on my plate, because I could be starving in Canaan, but instead I'm eating at the King's table. So what if somebody else is able to get prime rib and another person is eating lobster while I have nothing but ground beef? I thank You, God, for the food I'm about to receive."

Have you learned to stop looking at what other people are doing and how they're getting blessed, and instead just thank God for what's on your plate? A truly grateful person confesses to others, "I can also thank God for what's on my plate, because I don't really deserve to be eating anything at all. When I look at the mess I've made of my life and the stuff I've done that's gone wrong, I'm grateful to God for blessing me by letting me sit at the table."

Whatever's going on in your life, you've got to be grateful for what's on your plate. It could always be worse. So praise

God and say, "Any way You bless me, I'll be satisfied. If you bless me on the job or with a business, if you bless me in the front or in the background, I'm grateful because I could have been dead. I don't deserve any of Your benefits, so I'm going to be thankful for what's on my plate."

Why is it so many people are concerned with what others are doing? The Enemy will start distracting you by making you compare yourself to others. Even if you go to your family reunion, and your relatives are bragging on your cousin who finished college at the top of his class, received a boatload of honors, and is being courted by headhunters — don't compare, don't compete, and don't complain. Even if your own mother chooses to put your cousin's graduation picture and copies of his certificates and awards on your family mantel, don't get discouraged.

Don't remind yourself that you're around the same age but that he's married with a house and children while you're still living at home with your parents. When you start to look at others' lives and feel bad because you're not where they are, or your life's plate is seemingly not as full and appealing as theirs, take heart. Understand that what's on your plate is something you have nothing to do with. Everybody has an assignment or allotment in life.

Now, sometimes you can bring blessing to your life, but sometimes God lifts whom He will. You should pray, "God, I don't want what's on their plate because I don't know what they're catching trying to keep it." Stop worrying about what folk are saying about you. If you get paranoid about what other people are saying and doing, you'll miss your blessing by agonizing about who's going to take it away from you.

And when you get to that point, the greatest freedom you can have is when you say, "Lord, not everyone is a celebrated basketball player, gospel great, or award-winning actor. But whatever You put on my plate is more than I deserve. I'm appreciative and grateful for it."

MAKE A QUALITY DECISION TO PROSPER

Genesis 45:25-28; 46:1

After a series of tests, Joseph finally revealed himself to his brother. He wanted them to go and get his father, whom he had not seen since he was seventeen. So the brothers went home to get their father and bring him back into Joseph's presence.

The challenge was that their father Jacob was truly up there in age — the Bible lists him as being 130 years old. He had lived in Canaan all of his life, because it was the land that had been promised to his grandfather, Abram, hundreds of years before, when God told him to leave Ur of the Chaldees and go to the land that He would show him.

When the brothers got home, they told Jacob about Joseph and how he ruled Egypt. Yet the elderly man was already walking in and possessing what God had promised to his grandfather three generations earlier. Because he had lived in that land for all of his days, he was settled and comfortable. But now he was at the point of decision, a crossroads. Would Jacob stay where he was or heed the suggestion of his sons to go to Egypt? Would he be stretched to do something different, or would he refuse?

Jacob could have said, "You know what? I'm too old to learn something new. I'm good where I am. I don't want to try anything different. Please don't bother me, because I'm comfortable where I am."

You know how it is when you're set in your ways and it's hard to make a change. What happens in your life when you're being called from one area to another? What happens when you're comfortable in what seems to be your promised land, yet you feel as if you're being challenged to do something different? What happens when God is calling you to relocate?

What happens when you've been comfortable as a single woman for so long, and now some man has asked for your hand in matrimony? What do you do? What is the proper process for making a decision about a job, family, finances, a major purchase, or relocation? What about going back to school, starting your own business, beginning a family, or just doing something different? What do you do about life when you've been challenged to make a critical decision, but you're comfortable where you are?

If Jacob chose to stay in Canaan, his livestock, family, and everyone associated with him would die because of a lack of food. Yet even though it was a dysfunctional place, it was all Jacob knew. He was being called to leave what he was comfortable with and go somewhere else. He didn't know if it was better for him to just die or to 'move with the cheese', as a popular '90s motivational book puts it.

Should he 'join God where God is at work', as two notable Bible scholars have asked? Should he stay in a place where he's dying — where pellagra, malnutrition, and starvation are the order of the day — because he's been there so long, even though there is another possibility of supply waiting for him?

Have you ever been in a place of lack, starvation, and dysfunction, but because you've been there so long and you're comfortable there, sometimes you think it's just better for you to die where you are? Did you ever consider that God may be calling you to go somewhere else and do something else?

I know of people who have attended the same church for decades, even though they're starving spiritually and not being fed because their grandparents were among the first members. If I were to leave the Atlanta area today and return to the church in which I was raised, it would be as if I'd never left. There would be the same order of worship and the same prayers. Most members have been attending for so long they have gotten extremely comfortable there.

If this strikes a chord, you may be that person who doesn't want others to think badly of you, so you stay in a church when your heart is leading you elsewhere. You stay because you don't have the courage or faith to do anything different. But when God is calling you from glory to glory and faith to faith, you have to get to the point where you say to yourself, "My soul is too valuable. What does it profit me if I gain everything but die of spiritual starvation?"

Why are there men and women who allow themselves to become victims of domestic violence? Believe it or not, they've become comfortable in their victimization. Why do such people mistakenly call what they're going through 'their cross to bear'? When Jesus said in the Word to 'take up your cross daily,' He was not talking about allowing yourself to be physically abused. There's something terribly wrong when a person who knows and trusts God would rather stay in a dysfunctional relationship than live victoriously by themselves. You would think the time would come when they would say, "I understand that God has something better for me. I understand that I shouldn't die in this place when there are glorious opportunities waiting for me."

And so Jacob was at a critical place in his life. He had to make a decision. Was he going to die in a depraved, dysfunctional place of starvation?

Like Jacob, you may have concluded that decision-making is just an arbitrary process. Maybe you don't truly know how to properly make decisions about your life. Did you know that there is a formula for decision-making? In fact, those who deal with project management often refer to the 'science of decision-making'. This process ultimately involves identifying, determining, implementing, evaluating, monitoring, and, yes, making a decision.

You can't allow yourself to experience the 'paralysis of analysis'. Have you ever known people who have identified the problem, determined the alternatives, but spend time evaluating but never acting? Figure out what is the most appropriate alternative, and then make a decision. This process can be utilized even if you've just been diagnosed with a disease. Whenever you're trying to move to another place in life, the 'science of decision-making' will greatly benefit you.

What you'll discover is that in this passage, as we deal with the life of Jacob, he was engaged in the decision-making process. He did several key things that all of us must do when we're trying to either make a decision or help another person implement one.

Realize That You Must be Sensible

When you're making a decision, you've got to use your head. In other words, the decision has to make sense.

In Genesis 45, there was a famine in the lands of Canaan and Egypt. The only place Jacob's family could get food was Egypt, and that was miles and miles away. Eventually, they discovered who Joseph was, what he did, and how he could help them, especially in the area of food distribution. Eventually, they not only came to understand who their brother and son was, but *whose* he was. His willingness to forgive them for the wrong they had perpetrated against him more than two decades earlier showed him to be a man of God.

Even though Joseph's father was most likely struggling with leaving the only place he had ever known, he still realized that he had to be sensible. And so Jacob's charge was this: If he stayed in Canaan, he would die, along with his offspring and livestock. But if they died, the Bible would never get to David, which means we'll never get to Solomon, which means we'll never get to Joseph, which means we'll never get to Mary, which means we'll never get to Jesus. Of course it goes without saying, that will never happen, but Jacob had no earthly idea of the future. He had no idea that if he stayed there, his wrong decision would have universal ramifications for godly legacy and Christ would not have been born. As we look back, we see that he had no choice but to be sensible and use his head.

As you may well imagine, Jacob had a hard time accepting the fact that his beloved son was not only alive, but was chief cook and bottle-maker in Egypt. As mentioned earlier, if it's in the Word, it can manifest in your world. God is well able to resurrect what you thought was a thing of the past. After they told him what Joseph said, the Bible says that Jacob's spirit came back to him. Finally, the old man, who was set in his ways, decided that he had heard enough and would go to Egypt to see his long-lost son.

Be Transparent About Your Condition

You have to be sensible about where you are. If what you're doing is not working, has not worked, and there's no promise that it will ever work, you've got to be transparent about it. You must realize that the definition of insanity is when you do something over and over the same way each time and expect different results. At some point in your life, you have to be wise enough to try something different.

If you're struggling to make ends meet because you decided that you wouldn't work for anyone but yourself, it may be time to try something different. It seems as if every other month you come up with a new money-making scheme. This month you're selling vacation packages. Last month you were selling long-distance services. Not too long ago you were selling cellular phone service. After that, you were promoting a mid-level marketing program. When people ask you what you do, you proudly tell them you're an entrepreneur. Truth be told, you're not living up to your responsibility as a husband and father and are content to allow your wife to be the primary, consistent breadwinner.

You have to get to the point where you say, "I've got big dreams, but right now my dreams are not enough to help pay the mortgage. So let me get a lawnmower or go to McDonald's and find something I can do in the meantime. I'm not giving up on my dreams, but I must help bring some money into the house during the process until my dream materializes."

Like I said, you've got to be sensible at some point. Often, we make decisions without evaluating where we are in life and admitting that what we're doing is not working. We're all human beings, and we all struggle with our issues. It pains me to see Christians making wrong decisions. I'll be the first to tell you, if you ask me, that what you're doing is just not working.

Have you ever noticed that some of the most beautiful, successful young women in Hollywood jump from relationship to relationship, even though they get hurt each time they get involved with someone? Now, if you've dated seven people in three years, and each relationship went sour, at some point you've got to consider that you're choosing wrong or that, ultimately, the problem lies with you.

Moving from one relationship to another was the problem for the woman at the well. If only someone would e-mail this Scripture from the Book of John to some of those high-paid actresses and reality stars. I'm sure you know it well. Jesus went to a place called Sychar of Samaria and sat by a well. A woman got there around noon and Jesus asked her for drink of water.

She asked, "How is it that You, being a Jew, ask me, a Samaritan woman, for a drink? Don't you know that Jews don't have any dealings with Samaritans?"

Jesus said, "If you knew who it was that was asking you for a drink, you wouldn't let Me ask you for a drink. You'd be asking Me for a drink." Then He cut to the chase and told her to call her husband. She told Him she had no husband. He replied that she had five husbands and was then living with yet another man. He let her know that her life would be complete since she had met Him.

When will *you* mature to the point where you can recognize that if you keep doing the same things, you'll get the same awful results? You have to realize at some point that, like Jacob, if you stay in that wrong place, you're surely going to (figuratively) die.

Surround Yourself With Trusted Companions

Thank God that Jacob had enough sense to be transparent about his conditions. He also had some trusted companions. His sons had been to Egypt twice to survey the land. They had met with Joseph and had been in his house. So they brought Jacob word that the son he thought dead was, in fact, in Egypt. They convinced him to pack up and move forward. And even though Jacob's sons were younger and less experienced than he was, had he not trusted them enough to take their advice, he would have died in his stubbornness.

Make sure that when you are at crossroads, you don't get the wrong people involved in your decision-making process. Stop talking and telling your business to people who haven't been anywhere, seen anything, accomplished anything, or dealt with serious life issues. Pray something like this, in Jesus' name: "God, put people in my life whom I can trust to help me think through stuff because they have a different perspective. If I'm the smartest person in my group, I'm getting ready to die. Let me have somebody around who can sharpen and encourage me."

How is it that so many single women can give so much marital advice? In church (or elsewhere), you'd better be careful about those who say they have a word from God for you, especially those who try to tell you to leave the man you're with. You'd better make sure that every spirit talking to you is of God. If you mess around and leave your man and then come back two weeks later, the one with the 'godly' advice just may be in your house, wearing your bathrobe. You'd better ask God to show you which people to have around to help you through your decision-making processes.

Recognize That You Can't Act Out of Emotion

"It is enough. My son Joseph is alive. I will go and see him before I die," (Genesis 45:28). In other words, "So Joseph knows I'm getting up in age. I'm going to see him. My other sons have told me that we've got to go to Egypt."

> *"And Israel [Jacob] took his journey with all that he had."* (Genesis 46:1)

Ladies, I'm talking directly to you now. Because you've had some overnight trips at your boyfriend's house, perhaps you've (consciously or subconsciously) left some of your things there. Now you've broken up, but you left your phone in his name. You also left your tablet and shoes in his closet. Even though you got angry and headed for the door, still you left some stuff behind. The problem is that you shouldn't have been over there in the first place, but that's the subject of another book.

Now you're playing games with your emotions. You're moving on, but you're still leaving some stuff behind. Woman of God, let me tell you something. When God has spoken to your spirit and told you it's time for another day, it isn't time to play with the Devil. You've got to take everything you've got and say, "This chapter of my life is closed. I'm moving on, and I'm not going back." Only a dog comes back to his own vomit, but so many of us are coming back to those things that aren't good for us. There are things that God has delivered us from, but because we're acting out of our emotions, we get entangled in those messes all over again. So when you make a decision to end a relationship, stick with your God-inspired decision.

Some Christians, who ought to know better, are way too emotional. Someone on your job says something that offends you and you're on like a light. "I don't have to take this!" you shout. "Here's my resignation!" Then you get mad, pack up your stuff, and drive off. About halfway home, it hits you, "I haven't got a job. I only have two weeks' worth of savings in my bank account. My wife isn't working. My children need shoes." But because you've acted out of your emotions, you've lost your job.

How many people say regretful words to their spouses out of emotion? You get angry with your husband and tell him you should never have married him, that you should have stayed with your previous love. But then two months later you begin to wonder why his touch isn't quite the same. You've got to understand that when you put a word out into the atmosphere, that word can wound and harm someone. And once that hurtful word is gone from your lips, you can apologize, but it can never truly be taken back.

I'll never forget a time when my wife and I were first married. My sister called crying and saying that her boyfriend had assaulted her in the course of an argument. Now, pastor or not, no man is going to get away with beating up on any woman in my family. Immediately I reacted as if I was a pit bull. Enraged and full of emotion, I looked for any weapon I could get my hands on. My wife tried unsuccessfully to calm me down. Some man had just hit my sister, and there was no calming me at that point.

When I got to my sister's house, I knew that the situation was not going to be a pretty one. Hours earlier, I was anointed by the Holy Spirit to preach a word from God to my congregation, but this situation had nothing to do with the pulpit. This was family.

Before I could do any damage that required ammunition or a blade, her boyfriend walked toward me and asked me to wait a minute before I did something we would both regret. I calmed down long enough to ask him what had happened. He explained that my sister had said something derogatory and hurtful about his man parts; then she added that she should have stayed with her former lover because he could carnally satisfy her. Part of the problem was that they were shacked up, not married.

Not that I would ever condone domestic violence, but as a man, I could see why he was insulted enough to overact. There are just some things, ladies, that you should never say to your man. I returned home without committing the bodily harm that I had intended. Thank God that I am a new creature in Christ, getting closer daily to who the Word says I am.

The point I'm making here is that sometimes you can act out of your emotions when you don't even have the whole story. You make an assumption based on what you think you heard. Even the Bible tells us to hear the conclusion of the whole matter.

Remember That You Must be Spiritual

Jacob *". . . came to Beersheba, and offered sacrifices unto the God of his father Isaac,"* (Genesis 46:1). He went to worship God in the same place where his father had worshipped earlier in Genesis. Jacob must have been saying to himself, "God, You know I feel that I'm doing the right thing. I've analyzed the situation. I truly believe that if we stay here in Canaan, we're going to die. I trust my sons. They told me that Joseph is in Egypt. I've got trusted companions through whom I believe

You're going to speak to me. I've packed all of my stuff. I'm not going to act emotionally and vacillate. When I go, I'm going wholeheartedly. I'm putting everything into it."

"But God, here's my main problem: Even though I've got my own vision and plan and it feels right, I haven't talked to You about it yet. Let me get to Beersheba, where I can worship and offer sacrifices to You. Let me seek Your face, because even though I think it's the right thing, and although I trust the people who told me to leave Canaan and go to Egypt, I still haven't gotten away to commune with You."

It's possible for us to have good ideas, but not God ideas. It may make sense or seem like the right thing to do, but don't ever take that for granted, even if trusted people around you say it's right. You've got to get away to your version of Beersheba. Go to the sacred place where your forefathers prayed, even if it's only a figurative journey.

Say something like this to Him: "God, I'm on my way. I feel good about this, but I'm not going to make a decision based on the research I got off the Internet, or because my manager or publicist said this is what I should be doing. Before I sign this contract and buy this house, before I do anything, I'm going to get my facts together first, because faith without works is dead. I've packed up my stuff, but before I make my final decision, let me get away and spend some time in Beersheba."

Some of you would not have married your present (or former) spouse had you just spent some time in your version of Beersheba. Even some who took a job making what they happily believed was thousands of dollars' worth of increased joy, but got thousands more headaches, wouldn't have taken the job had they spent even a little time in prayer. You need to pray, "God, don't let me ever get caught up in who said this and who recommended that. I need to get myself to Beersheba and stay there until I get a specific word from You."

We've all had situations where someone hurt our feelings and made us angry. We were irritated and upset. And sometimes, when we hear things, we have to decide whether we're hearing God or just our emotions. When we have a dream, vision, or desire to do something, we must conclude whether or not we're following our own personal agenda or hearing from God.

It may be difficult to discern on your own. Moses acted out of his emotions and hit the rock. His spiritual nature was trying to speak to him, but because he acted out of his emotions, he prevented himself from getting to the Promised Land. I know you think you're wise, but don't make any major decision in your life without seeking God first.

Jacob went and talked with God in Beersheba, and God turned around and talked to him. *"And God spake to Israel [Jacob] and said, Jacob, Jacob. And he said, Here am I. And he said, I am God, the God of your father."* In Hebrew, that means 'the God who deserves the name'. *"Fear not to go down into Egypt; for I will there make of thee a great nation."* The next verse says, *"I will go down with thee into Egypt."*

God was saying, "Jacob, I promise that if you do this, I'm going to turn you into a great nation." But here is also the promise of God's protection: "Jacob, if you go, I'm going to go with you."

That's good news. When God has given you a word and spoken revelation over your life, the greatest deliverance is knowing that you're not going by yourself. We have a God who had promised that He'll go with us. When He sends you, you're never alone.

Perhaps, like Jacob, you're caught between Canaan and Egypt. You have a major life decision facing you. Maybe you have to decide whether to undergo chemotherapy or relocate to another part of the country because you received a job offer. It may involve signing divorce papers or going back to school. At one time in my life, I operated out of fear because I didn't know what the outcome of my decisions would be. Now, when I have to make a major decision, this is how I can sleep at night.

Proverbs 3:5-6 says, *"Trust in the Lord with all of thine heart and lean not unto thine own understanding. In all thy ways acknowledge Him, and He shall direct your path."*

Personal Agenda or God's Divine Plan?

Genesis 49:33; 50:1

After twenty-five years, Joseph reconciled with the brothers who had sold him into slavery. He also saw his father, Jacob. The lands of Canaan and Egypt had both been overrun by famine and extreme recession. God used Joseph to provide food for all those who lived in Goshen, Egypt, and Canaan. The dream that he'd had when he was seventeen had materialized.

The dream had been preordained for him in much the same way God spoke about the prophet's mission in Jeremiah 1:5, *"Before I formed you in the belly of your mother, I knew you. I sanctified you, and I had already ordained you to be a prophet to the nations."* That same type of providence was prepared for Joseph before he was born.

This is how I imagine things went down: Jacob went to his prospective wife, Rachel, and asked for her hand in marriage. She consented, and they 'knew' each other and produced Joseph. But even before God allowed Jacob and Rachel to intertwine, He had already preordained that Joseph would be imbued with his famous dream. That's why Paul said in Romans 8:29-30, *"For whom he did foreknow, he also did predestinate. . . he also justified. . . he also glorified."*

The good news is that he knew his brothers finally understood that before Joseph ever had a dream, God had already arranged that one day what He had spoken out loud would be manifested. No matter where you are in life, what God has providentially and prophetically spoken over your life will eventually come to pass — come hell or high water, come family members who are rebellious, come those who pat you on the back to either give you accolades, applause, or to find a soft spot to stick a knife in you.

Regardless of everything you've been through, I want you to know that *"He who hath begun a good work in you will be faithful to complete it in you."* If God said it, it will come to pass. You should thank God that every dream He has placed in your heart will come to fruition. Jesus is the Author and Finisher of our faith. He is Alpha who has no beginning, and He will be there when we get to Omega.

Talk often revolves around Joseph's life being actualized by a dream, yet there are sections of Genesis that touch on what may have been his worst nightmare. I'm not talking about his brothers' betrayal, his Egyptian enslavement, the accusation made by Potiphar's wife about sexual impropriety, imprisonment in Potiphar's jail, or the famished and arid conditions that came to Canaan, Egypt, and Goshen. No, Joseph's worst nightmare happened after being separated from his father.

Jacob was not there to encourage, teach, support, or train him throughout his life. He had to become a man on his own. At the time when Joseph needed his father the most — the one he loved and the one who loved him — he had instead been separated from him for more than two decades. After being without his father all those years, Joseph was robbed of many earthly experiences with his father. But at last, he was finally able to enjoy reconnecting with his father, who in turn got to spend time with his grandchildren. His father was, at that point in his life, able to give Joseph final instructions before his death.

Jacob, according to Scripture, spoke a word of wisdom over each of his sons and then closed his eyes, and his voice was hushed by that common denominator of us all — death. The dreamer experiences what must have been the most difficult moment of his earthly sojourn — his father had died. The one who had given him a reason to dream and believe was gone.

Who was Joseph going to call now? He no longer had a father, mother, or grandfather. Who was he going to depend upon? What was he going to do? If you've enjoyed the comfort, convenience, and assurance of a relationship with your parents, you're faced with a dilemma when you can no longer pick up the phone and call them ever again. Oh, what we'd say if we could have but one more conversation with someone we love who has gone on to be with the Lord.

As your children grow up and become teenagers, you sometimes don't know what to do with them. You'd give anything to be able to pick up the phone and call your parents and ask them how they handled you when you were going through the teenage years. Recently, I spoke with a member of my congregation about a mutual friend who is also a great musician, producer, and pastor. This friend's father was a retired preacher who turned church duties over to his son, like when things transitioned from Moses to Joshua. On the subject of being a new pastor, our friend mentioned to his father that since he had never officiated over a funeral before, he would more than likely be at a loss when that time came. You see, although his father had just retired, this new pastor still depended on his dad's wisdom and guidance. The day after that conversation, his father passed away.

What do you do when you're excited about the possibilities of your new season, but you still long for the security of those upon whose shoulders you stand? And now you've got to do it all by yourself. Now you've got to make all the decisions. What do you do when you're enjoying your dream, at the peak of your prosperity and popularity, and all of a sudden the bottom drops out? You're living in your dream but temporarily experiencing a nightmare.

What do you do when you're riding high with a lot of money and a great career, but all of a sudden your dream turns into your worst nightmare? If you're not careful, you can run into some difficult circumstances in your life that will take the breath out of you and make you throw your hands up in the classic gesture of despair. That's what happened to Joseph. He had been a dreamer, but this was a nightmare.

Perhaps things are running smoothly right now and you've reached a great place in your life. Maybe you're good. You and your spouse are of one accord, and you're enjoying peace and harmony on the job. The stocks in your portfolio are earning more dollars for you every day, enhancing your upward mobility. Perhaps the message of this chapter isn't for you, but I guarantee that life will eventually throw something at you. At some point, you'll have to take this word out of the freezer, thaw it out, and apply it to your life.

Joseph had a nightmare, but there are three major things you can learn from his experience that will benefit you when you are undergoing a difficult time in your own life.

Resolve Not to Over-spiritualize Your Burdens

Jacob finished talking with his sons and gave them a final blessing. After speaking a word to each one of them, he pulled his feet into the bed, lay his head on the pillow, and breathed his last breath.

"And Joseph fell upon his father's face, and wept upon him, and kissed him." When Joseph's father died, he accepted the reality of his death. He did not try mouth-to-mouth resuscitation on his dad, or request that time period's version of a doctor to try to revive him. Instead, Joseph said through his gesture that his father's death was inevitable and acceptable. Since there was nothing to be done about it, Joseph didn't over-dramatize by using pious words when simple ones would do.

He wept and then went to Pharaoh and told him that his father had just died. He wasn't trying to deal with this drama by himself. When some of us go through situations, we become insular by not letting people know what we're dealing with. Instead, we try to act as if we're strong because we don't want to give the impression to others that we're vulnerable or weak.

But things will happen in life that prompt you to find someone who loves you and respects you, to share with them whatever it is you're dealing with. Everyone needs someone they can talk to, especially when they're going through difficult situations.

Men are prone to think they're so strong that they don't need to talk to a counselor for fear of telling another person about their business. But because you internalize what you're going through, you end up imploding. Sometimes you have to schedule an appointment to talk with someone to keep from losing your perspective and balance. You need to talk to someone you can trust to share what you're going through. Stop saying, "I'm just going to fake it 'til I make it," and stop acting like everything's good when a loved one dies. You've got to deal with the facts.

Joseph took time to air out his feelings. *"Arriving at the Atad Threshing Floor just across the Jordan River, they stopped for a period of mourning, letting their grief out in loud and lengthy lament. For seven days, Joseph engaged in these funeral rites for his father."* Contrary to popular opinion, besides its use in farming, in ancient times the threshing floor was not a place of worship, but of mourning.

You know what the problem is for many of us? Sometimes when death comes, we stay busy doing routine things so we won't have to think about it. But when the painful inevitabilities of life give you negative and bitter emotions, you'd better stop at some point and go somewhere to be alone. If you've got to take off your makeup or lace-front first, fine, but find some time to be alone and just let it out.

Joseph must have had some African blood in him, because traditionally, people of color are known to grieve long and loud. I'm speaking from family experience, not of an entire race. If you've been to an African-American funeral, you know what I'm talking about. Joseph let out the grief and pain he felt with loud and long crying. Too many people try to over-spiritualize and end up not being real. If this describes you, be careful. If you don't let those painful, negative emotions out, you may end up hurting yourself more.

Take care not to try to handle emotional pain on your own with coping mechanisms that merely anesthetize you so you'll temporarily feel better. I'm talking about substances used to numb your pain or drown out what's already on the inside. When you've got inner demons and internal pain, the worst thing you can do is self-medicate. Go somewhere to be alone and acknowledge the pain. Then lay it at the feet of Jesus. Stop holding the pain inside. Let it go!

Men especially seem to feel as if we have to keep all the bad stuff inside, that expressing emotions and crying are signs of weakness. Men, I submit to you that this is why women live longer than we do. We think they're weak, vulnerable, and unstable because they cry, put their hands on their hips, wag their fingers, and roll their necks around. But what looks like attitude to you is actually a way of letting the emotions of the situation out.

Statistics show that men tend to keep their emotions bottled up inside, and they suffer premature death as a result. It almost seems as if we men shouldn't be forced to pay into Social Security because we don't live long enough get benefits. (Of course, as Christians, we obey the law of the land. I'm just saying . . .) When you're going through something, strength comes when you let it all out and say, "Yes, I'm going through stuff, but it's not going to take me out because 'Greater is He that is in me than He that is in the world.' "

Don't Be Overcome by Bondage

Many of you spend your time on the weekend focused on the winning lottery numbers to see if you hit the jackpot, but you can win hundreds of millions and still have things in your life that are not good. Money can buy a nice house, but it can't buy you a home. Money can buy health insurance, but it can't buy health and strength. Money can buy an alarm clock, but it can't wake you up in the morning. Money can buy physical intimacy, but it can't buy you love. There are just some things that money can't buy.

The text says it took Joseph nearly forty days to embalm his dad. Then he conducted seven different funerals. He was at a place in his life where all his money couldn't bring his father back. He dealt with his feelings and let them out. He lamented at length, and then, *They took [Jacob] to Canaan and buried him in the cave. . . in the plot of Ephron the Hittite. After burying his father, Joseph went back to Egypt.*

He took off at least two months, a season, to get himself together and let out his feelings. I've known those who ended a relationship at the beginning of the month and got involved in another by the next two-week pay period. Resolve to take time to deal with the pain of an emotional breakup before you move on to someone new. Close one chapter before you start another one.

It's okay to let your feelings out and take some time to deal with them, but you have to get to the point where you say it's time to move on. Tell yourself that it's time to get back to the land of the living. How long are you going to mourn? How long are you going to be hurt by something you can't change? Get back in the fight. Get your life, job, joy, and peace of mind back.

Surely you know people who, after years of trying, can't come to grips with the fact that the one they want just doesn't love them. What does that song say? "I can't make you love me if you don't." Accept that reality. Even while you were with that person, they showed a lack of interest in your well-being. Deal with the rejection and then say, "I'm going to bury this relationship. I'm not going to stay bound by the old season, and I'm destroying anything, such as pictures, that remind me of them."

Tell yourself, "I'm going to get myself together. I'm going to fix up the house. I'm going to the gym to do Pilates. I'm going to get a new hairdo, and I'm going to reinvent myself." Take good care of yourself when you're trying to regroup from a painful situation.

God Can Overturn Your Situation

When Joseph went back to Egypt, his brothers started talking amongst themselves after their father had died. They surmised that Joseph may be angry and possibly in the mood to seek revenge for when they sold him into slavery. They concluded that the only reason he hadn't acted against them earlier was that their father was still alive.

Isn't it interesting how, in the beginning of the story, they were big and bad enough to throw him into a pit, but at this point they resorted to sending one of Joseph's servants to deliver a message? When they asked for forgiveness and told Joseph their dad would have wanted it that way, he cried. He sent for them, and when they came, he assured them that he wasn't angry and that he had no intention of killing them. He let them know that although what they had done to him was meant for evil, he was happy to say that God overturned the bad they had planned and that Joseph had benefitted.

Perhaps you've been dealing with a personal nightmare of your own. Just remember: If He did it for one, He'll do it for all. The God you serve can most assuredly turn bad things around for your good.

That's why Paul says in 2 Corinthians 12:9, *"Most gladly, therefore, would I rather glory in my infirmities that the power of Christ may rest upon me. For when I am weak, then am I strong."*

David put it this way in Psalm 27:1-3: *"The Lord is my light and my salvation; whom shall I fear? The Lord is the strength of my life; of whom shall I be afraid? When my enemies and foes came upon me, they stumbled and fell. Though the enemy encamp about me, I shall not fear."*

If you are imbued with a dream and subsequently faced with a nightmare situation, remember to wait on the Lord and be of good courage, and the Lord will strengthen your heart.

In August 2005, Hurricane Katrina came through the Gulf of Mexico and then Lake Pontchartrain, taking direct aim on the 9th Ward section of New Orleans. There was massive flooding, destruction of life and property, multi-family displacement, and social and political chaos. And as with most tragedies, there are tales of heroism, bravery, and outright miracles.

The story goes that there was a senior-aged female who was raising her grandson in what is known as a shotgun house, so narrow and small that if you opened the front door, you could fire a shotgun and the bullet would go straight out the back door. To put it nicely, the house was in a state of disrepair even before the storm hit. Under hurricane-force winds, the house was totally destroyed. Word has it that she and her grandson clung to the roof for several days and nights, waiting for help to arrive. And it did, in the form of a FEMA-produced bus.

First they went to temporary shelter at the city convention center, and then on to the safety of Atlanta, Georgia. Her dreams for upward mobility and a better life for her grandson were as battered as her former house had been. She had no idea how they would survive (But God knew). The old woman was blessed enough to encounter philanthropists who gave her a job and awarded her grandson a full scholarship at Morehouse College. And that's not all. Those angels of God, in the form of benefactors, set her up in a brand-new house of her own.

Maybe you're going through your own brand of Hell, but I've got good news for you. We've all had sorrow. There were times in my life when I faced sorrow and troubles. But in each trial and tribulation, God gave me blessed consolation. He let me know that the trials only come to make me strong. So I thank God for the mountains and the valleys. I thank Him for the storms He's brought me through, because if I never had a problem, I would never know that God can solve whatever problem comes my way. I wouldn't know what faith in God's Word can do. Through it all, I've learned to trust in Jesus. Through it all, I've learned to trust in God.

Hopefully, you can trust in God to know when you're hearing directly from Him about what you should do with your life — or whether or not you're self-absorbed with your own agenda. God will give you the desires of your heart. Child of God, know that if the desires come from Him, you will have all the finances, support, and favor you need to succeed. Because when God gives you a dream and speaks to your spirit about a vision for your life, He makes provision. That's how you know that the plan for your life is endorsed by God and destined to succeed.